Kiss and Tell

THE ESSENTIAL WORKTEXT ON HOW TO WRITE A ROMANCE

written by

Rita-award Winning, Best-selling Romance Author

Susan May Warren

 Published by My Book Therapy, a division of Susan May Warren Fiction, LLC, PO Box 1290, Grand Marais, MN 55604. First Edition.

Visit our Web site at www.mybooktherapy.com for information on more resources for writers.

To receive instruction on writing or further help with writing projects via My Book Therapy's boutique fiction editing services, contact info@mybooktherapy.com

My special thanks go to Beth Vogt, for her endless hours of editing.

Dedicated to:

Andrew Warren for showing me what it means to love someone.

For your Glory, Lord

Table of Contents

Susan May Warren

is the award-winning, bestselling author of over thirty novels. A four-time Christy award finalist and a RITA finalist, she is a multi-time winner of the Inspirational Reader's Choice contest and the ACFW Carol Award, and was the 2010 ACFW Mentor of the Year. She specializes in characterization and has won acclaim for her gripping stories and suspenseful plots. Susan teaches on writing at conferences around the nation.

A Note from your Therapist

I love romance. My boys are convinced I am a hopeless romantic, from the way I make them learn to dance (yes, I'm a firm believer that every boy should know a few foxtrot and swing dance steps) to the advice I give them on dating. A small part of me lives in that happy world where people break out into song, make grand gestures for each other, and say deep, profound, romantic things.

And I'm not the only one who loves romance. The romance genre continues to hold strong despite the recession. According to the 2008 Romance Writers of America (RWA) annual report, romance fiction generated $1.37 billion in sales and remained the **largest share of the consumer market** at 13.5 percent. The romance genre continues to dominate the publishing world. The truth is, people still want to believe in love and happily ever after, even in the bad times. Maybe *especially* in the bad times.

It behooves us then, as writers, to consider romance as we write our novels. Whether we're die hard romantics who want to write a full-out romance, or romantic suspense writers who write half and half, or even women's fiction, fantasy, or thriller writers who add just a smidge of romance, there's no doubt that a great romance thread makes a good story great. Even men like a little romance. (I have a growing list of male readers who swear me to secrecy!)

So, how *do* you write a great romance? **It's all about creating great expectations!**

Not long ago, my husband and I celebrated twenty years of marriage. Since I was doing a book tour in Holland, we decided to add on a trip to Prague. About four months before our trip, we got online and searched for hotels and found a beautiful hotel right on Old Town Square, facing the Tyn Cathedral. We ordered Prague travel books and we hired a guide for a day. My husband recorded every travel channel episode he could find on Prague, which led to a day-long excursion to find the perfect apple strudel, thank you so much, Samantha Brown.

We were ready. Or so we thought.

We knew from pictures that it was beautiful, but when our taxi drove us into Old Town square, words failed us. Everything—from the dark grandeur of the gothic cathedral, to the storybook buildings bordering the square, to the tangy smell of the local café ovens roasting pork the fresh bouquet of linden trees, to the sound of horses' hooves clopping across black cobblestones—convinced us that we'd been swept into a fairytale. We expected to eat a pig's knuckle, explore castles, to linger at the artwork and sculptures on St. Charles Bridge, to tour the city, and most of all, to escape into a different and romantic culture. Our anticipation only whetted our appetite, and the reality exceeded our expectations.

A great romance novel does exactly this. We understand the feelings of falling in love, but a great romance brings these feelings to life and stirs in us those memories and moments we may have forgotten. A romance captures the hope and anticipation and, most of all, that sense of intimate belonging we all crave.

But what sets a romance apart from, say, a literary novel? Or even women's fiction?

A great romance is comprised of loveable heroes and heroines we want to root for. It's about tension and sexual sparks (even in inspirational romances). A great romance woos the reader with dialogue and creative scenes (not unlike dating!). It has a Black Moment and an Epiphany, and especially a happily ever after. A great romance is about meeting expectations. When a story lets you down, it's because it didn't meet one of the essential storycrafting expectations.

Because of that, all romances have the same ten elements. And yes, it's a formula, but just like perfumes are formula, when they are put together differently, they create a different scent. Your novel may use a formula, but only you can create it, adding your own unique "fragrance."

In *Kiss and Tell*, I'm going to reveal my secret ten ingredients and demystify the romance formula. I'll walk you through questions as you create your hero and heroine, then we'll apply these ten ingredients into the structure of a three act romance structure. Finally, you'll learn some techniques, some lethal weapons, and what to do after you novel is written.

Are you ready to fall in love?

THE 10 INGREDIENTS OF A ROMANCE

Take a romance off your shelf. It doesn't matter what subgenre it is—romantic suspense, historical romance, contemporary romance, Amish romance, vampire romance, supernatural romance, even erotica—the plot will have the same elements as every other romance. They may be in different order, but for your romance to have the right fragrance and to meet expectations, you'll need to recognize and apply these ten ingredients.

Boy Meets Girl – An event, goal, or circumstance occurs to bring our hero and heroine together.

Interest/Need – Something about their individual situations makes their hearts vulnerable to romance.

Why – The core reasons why they belong together.

Why Not – External and Internal Obstacles between the hero and heroine conspire to separate them.

Wooing – Events or situations that allow the hero and heroine to fall in love.

Sizzle – Dialogue that creates romantic tension.

Kiss – The romantic tension leads to the physical connection.

Breakup – The biggest Why Not (Obstacle) rises to push them apart and scrape open their wounds.

Make Up – The wound is healed and the Big Why (the core reason they belong together) saves the day.

Big Gesture/Sacrifice/HEA – The Hero or Heroine are able to prove their love through big gestures/sacrifices in order to stay together and find the love they've always longed for.

We'll go through each of these in upcoming chapters. However, if you are plotting a book, knowing this structure may assist you in laying out a rough plot. Before you even start your character study, you may brainstorm with these elements to see if you like the story, and if it works.

Real Life Example

Let's take a look at how these ten ingredients might work when you plot a book. Here's an example from the rough romance plotting I did on a recent category romance.

Boy Meets Girl – An event, goal, or circumstance occurs to bring our hero and heroine together

The hero and heroine are attending different weddings at the same location. They get into the same cab, mistaking each other for people they haven't met but are supposed to. The hero is an undercover security agent and is supposed to meet up with another agent, pose as her fiancé, and protect the bride. The heroine is supposed to be the maid of honor at her sister's wedding and is the blind date of one of the groomsmen.

Interest/Need = Why – Something about their individual situations makes their hearts vulnerable to romance

The heroine's sister is marrying the man whom the heroine loved. In fact, she believed the groom loved *her*. She is tired of living *outside* the romance novel and wants her own Happily Ever After (HEA).

The hero used to be a wild guy but has changed his ways. Now he's afraid to be with a woman because he doesn't know how to date a nice girl. But he wants someone he can love and trust, and someone who sees him as a hero.

Why – The core reasons why they belong together

They both value family, although in different ways, as well as honesty. She is reliable and he is surprised that he can trust her—although, for the first time in years, he *wants* to trust someone. And she trusts him, which makes him want to protect her.

The heroine enjoys being a "super spy" if only for a day. She feels like she is more than who she has become. And the fact that the hero is depending on her only makes her rise to the challenge. Finally, he makes her feel beautiful and not rejected.

Why Not – External and internal obstacles between the hero and heroine, as well as true love, conspire to separate them

The hero needs her to be his date to accomplish his mission. She feels like he tricked her and now trapped her into helping him. They don't trust each other.

Wooing – Events or situations allow the hero and heroine to fall in love

Despite being tricked, she agrees to help him, and her willingness to go out of her comfort zone allows him to get his job done. They are put into increasingly dangerous situations that allow their trust for each other to grow.

Because he has "tricked" her into helping him, he has to be kind to her, and charm her . . . and eventually start to be truly heroic as he responds to her.

Sizzle – Dialogue that creates romantic tension.

At first, their situation produces dramatic irony, as they are each talking about different weddings. Then, because they are supposed to be engaged, they are fighting even as they are trying to "get along." Finally, they have a staged fight . . . that leads to a real fight.

Kiss – The romantic tension leads to the physical connection.

They are supposed to be engaged, which causes them to be in "romantic" situations, including a fake kiss . . . that leads to real attraction.

Breakup – The biggest Why Not rises to push them apart and scrape open their wounds.

His mission is going to get an untrained person hurt. He can't fall for her because it will only distract him, not to mention that their real lives are vastly different. So, for the good of the mission, and her, he stages a cruel breakup. This fight embarrasses and hurts her, and she believes all his feelings for her were just an act (not unlike the feelings her ex- boyfriend-turned-future-brother-in-law).

Makeup – The wound is healed and the Big Why (the core reason they belong together) saves the day.

He's always wanted someone he can trust—and the fact that this non-agent went out of her way to help him gives him hope that there are people worth trusting. More than that, when she's tested, she protects his mission. She's exactly the kind of person he wants to be with—trustworthy, daring, and even fun.

She's always wanted a man who really wants her—who will fight for her and come after her. The hero is exactly this kind of guy when he realizes his feelings for her and begins to protect her instead of completing his mission.

Big Gesture/Sacrifice/HEA – The hero or heroine are able to prove their love through big gestures/sacrifice in order to stay together and find the love they've always longed for.

The heroine surrenders her hopes of getting back into her sister's good graces (and her wedding) in order to help the hero complete his mission. The hero stays with her after his mission is over and acts as her "plus one," proving to her sister and new husband that the heroine is not alone. (And c'mon, he's about a thousand times better than the guy who broke her heart.)

They ride off on a motorbike together . . . and maybe she's wearing a wedding dress. ☺

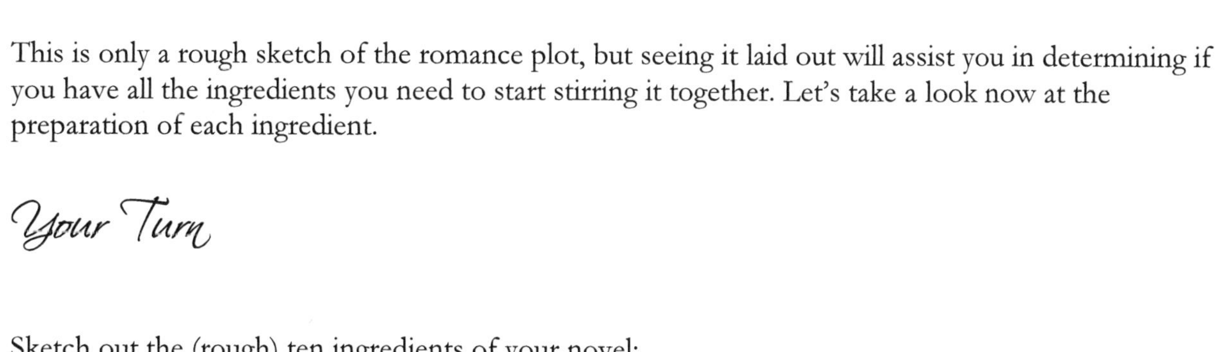

This is only a rough sketch of the romance plot, but seeing it laid out will assist you in determining if you have all the ingredients you need to start stirring it together. Let's take a look now at the preparation of each ingredient.

Your Turn

Sketch out the (rough) ten ingredients of your novel:

Boy Meets Girl – An event, goal, or circumstance occurs to bring our hero and heroine together.

Interest/Need – Something about their individual situations makes their hearts vulnerable to romance.

Why – The core reasons why they belong together.

Why Not – External and Internal Obstacles between the hero and heroine conspire to separate them.

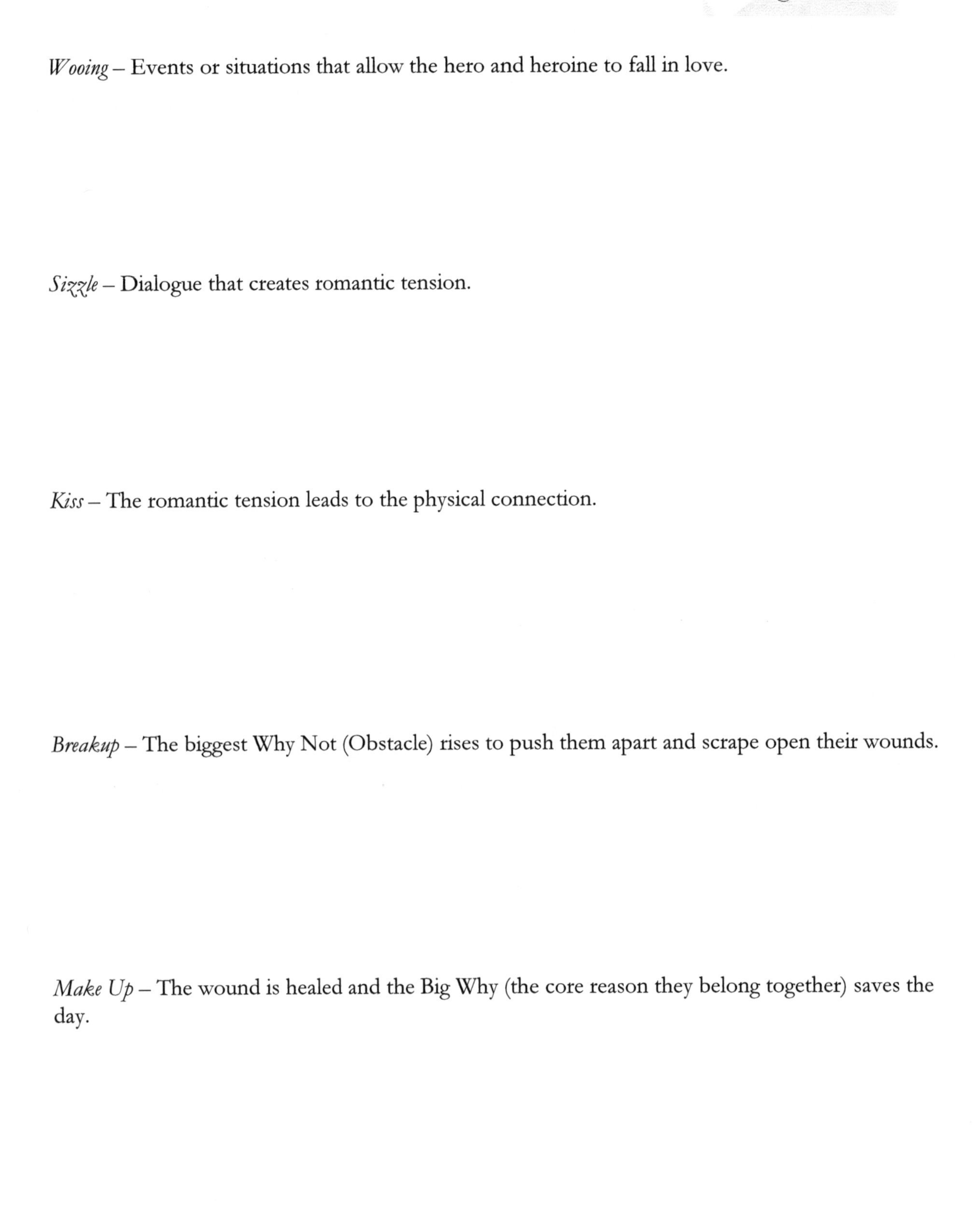

Wooing – Events or situations that allow the hero and heroine to fall in love.

Sizzle – Dialogue that creates romantic tension.

Kiss – The romantic tension leads to the physical connection.

Breakup – The biggest Why Not (Obstacle) rises to push them apart and scrape open their wounds.

Make Up – The wound is healed and the Big Why (the core reason they belong together) saves the day.

SECTION ONE: THE RECIPE

The Writing Process

Before we jump into the ten ingredients, let's take a moment to talk about the writing process. Most stories start out with an idea spark. A tidbit from life, or the news, or in your reading has ignited a story idea. We call this the premise, and it's enough to get you (and perhaps others) excited about your novel. But a story idea, or premise, does not a novel make, so now comes the hard work.

The first stage of novel crafting needs to be research into what publisher will be interested in your story. If you are a connoisseur of category romances—the mass market-size novels that are published every month from Harlequin—then you might consider writing one of those. Usually, they are 55K-60K words, have two points of view (POV)--the hero and heroine—and each particular "line" (Love Inspired Suspense, or Harlequin Intrigue are examples of "lines" within a publishing house) has their own particular guidelines. If you plan on writing a category romance, go to the publisher's website and download their writer's guidelines. It will give you the particulars on how to write for their particular line.

If you prefer a longer novel, longer mass market size, or trade size (the oversize books that are sold in bookstores rather than grocery store racks), then you are looking at a longer word count—something in the area of 75K-90K words. This length gives you the opportunity to develop a subplot, or add in a villain POV, as well as building in more conflict and romance.

Once you've decided the length and market for your romance, it's time to build your characters and start crafting the ten beats of your story. (We'll dive into these beats and character creation in a moment.) You may not want to plot out every nuance of your story, but if you give yourself a skeleton structure, you can then fill in the gaps as you write, discovering your story along the way. I highly recommend knowing the beats, however. It keeps writer's block from setting in and gives you a roadmap to your next destination in your plot.

Writing the story is about sitting down and working it out, scene by scene. I recommend a scene no shorter than 1200 words, and no longer than 3000. Your reader needs a break between reading and if your scenes are too long, they will become fatigued. Likewise, if your scenes are too short, you won't be able to establish all the scene elements necessary to affect the emotions of the reader (which is the point of the story). Often, a chapter has two scenes, although if the scenes are short, you might want to add a third scene.

Scenes are the glue that holds your plot together. We'll start with a look at the overall plot, but then we'll dissect it down to the essential scenes to include in your novel. Although we don't dive into full scene construction in this primer, information on how to craft a scene can be found at www.mybooktherapy.com.

Once your novel is finished, of course you'll edit it, get feedback from others, and then begin the process of selling it. Information on how to craft a proposal is included in the final section of this book.

Writing a novel is a profound, comprehensive undertaking. But if you break your novel down into ingredients it becomes manageable, even exciting as you journey through the romance of your characters.

Which is where we are going to start.

Ingredient 1: Boy Meets Girl

We fall in love with people, not events. Not plots. Not great storyworld, riveting dialogue, or prose. *People.* Characters who feel real and who we could actually meet. Characters with flaws and fears—and yet enough confidence to drive them through the story.

Characters who win our hearts.

How do you craft these kinds of romantic heroes and heroines? Let's start with our heart-throb hero.

Heroes

Every romance has to have a great hero who leaps off the screen and into our hearts. Think of your favorites: William Wallace in *Braveheart*, or maybe Robin Longstride in *Robin Hood.* Maybe it's simpler modern day hero like Hugh Grant in *Notting Hill.*

As you start building your romance, crafting the right hero is key. You need a man who will be noble, but flawed enough to be relatable because every woman wants to come to the aid of her man, just a little. (It's the nurturer inside of every woman.) He must also have a fear, something the author can put pressure on to make him behave. Finally, he must be courageous and willing to face those dark fears.

Let's take a closer look.

A Hero Must Be Noble. Every hero must have something to fight for. As Miracle Max says in *The Princess Bride*: "What do you have to live for?" The answer: True Love. Perhaps your hero isn't fighting for true love. (At least not at the beginning. By the end of the romance, he will be!) However, every hero must have something he believes in, something we find noble and true and worth believing in with him, even when he acts like a cad to the woman he loves. Maybe it's a secret, or a wish, or a past mistake. It could be a dream, or something he's protecting the heroine from. It could be his family, or his homeland.

Let's take a look at some of our favorite romances:
You've Got Mail: The hero, Joe, longs for the one woman who fills him with joy. (Remember what Joe says to his father on the boat?) He isn't a jerk—we know this because we see how he is kind to his siblings (or uncle, if you know the weird storyline). And he doesn't like how his father and grandfather have gone through women, marrying them and then divorcing them after affairs with the nannies. Our hero wants true love.

While You Were Sleeping: The hero, Jack, wants something—*someone*—of quality. Okay, Jack expresses it in making this amazing chair, but because of this, we see deeper into his heart. He isn't just a glitzy, shallow man like his brother Peter, the guy in the coma the heroine *thinks* she wants. The hero is a man who knows craftsmanship and quality. Most of all, he sees that in our heroine.

Sleepless in Seattle: Our hero, Sam, wants someone who completes him. Who complements him so well he doesn't know where his hand stops and hers begins. Sam wants the real thing—and we see that he is the real thing in how he relates to his son. He's a good father, and will be a good husband with the right woman who fits his life.

In *Chasing Liberty* (a lose remake of *Roman Holiday*), the hero is all about protecting the heroine, the daughter of the President.(We see this Noble Cause in a lot of movies, even *Notting Hill.*) However, Ben also wants a woman who will sacrifice what she wants in order to be with him. He wants the grand gesture—something he also gives her as he follows her through Europe.

Whatever your hero's Noble Cause is, it needs to be strong enough for us to love him and forgive him when he does something stupid. (Like in *You've Got Mail* when Joe Fox stands up Kathleen Kelly in the café.)

Book Therapy Question for your hero: What causes are you fighting for that make us love you?

Noble Cause versus Noble Moment:
Along with a Noble Cause, you will also craft a Noble Moment because although our hero may have a Noble Cause, he behaves poorly. And if he behaves too poorly, then we might reject him before we understand what he has to fight for.

This is solved by inserting a Noble Moment, aka, the "Boy Scout Moment" in the beginning of the novel. This is sometimes referred to as "Save the Cat" or "Pet the Dog." A Boy Scout Moment is when the hero does something noble and good—like save a cat, pet a dog, or help an old lady across the street—that shows us that he's a good guy. It's a glimpse of his nobility.

It's Jack Ryan in *The Hunt for Red October* kissing his daughter and packing her teddy bear in his briefcase.

It's Bob in *Return to Me* not betraying the waitress when she fills the bottle with tap water.

It's Sam in *Sleepless in Seattle* cuddling up with his son even after said son forces him to talk with a radio talk show host on Christmas Eve.

It's when, in *P.S. I Love You,* Gerry says in the middle of the fight, "Am I going to have to sleep in the tub again?" And then he dances in his underwear to make his wife smile.

The Boy Scout Moment is a small, yet memorable act, and building it into one of the early chapters of a book allows us to like the hero until his Noble Cause is apparent.

Book Therapy Question: What sweet, kind, and sacrificial Boy Scout Moment can you insert into the story early on to stir the reader's love for the hero?

Your hero must have a flaw.

Your hero must be less than perfect. Some characteristic that makes him real. Maybe he has issues with recklessness, or perhaps he trusts too much and has gotten burned. Maybe he's jaded and mean on the outside, but of course, he's tenderhearted on the inside. (However, though he's less than perfect, he's fixable.) A hero who is too good to be true is an untouchable hero, someone we find difficult to love.

Let's look at some of our favorite movies and their flawed heroes:

The Sleepless Flaw. This is where the hero is stymied and doesn't move forward and get the girl. We see this flaw in *While You Were Sleeping.* Jack refuses to tell his father that he doesn't want to be in the estate sale business anymore, and keeps his furniture building business a secret. He also doesn't want to "steal" his brother's fiancée, which is admirable, except that, well, we want him to speak up too! Jack's flaw is that he holds back when he should charge forward. We see this timid flaw played out in movies like *The Wedding Planner* or *Two Weeks' Notice.*

The Troublemaker Flaw. Like Johnny Castle in *Dirty Dancing*, this is where the hero is simply a bad influence on the heroine. We see this in movies like *Titanic*, where Jack's flaw is that he is a gambling vagabond, not good enough for our heroine. Of course, we see his true value, but he struggles with feeling that he doesn't deserve Rose. He is also a bit of a troublemaker and gets her into trouble as well. Again, we might find these characteristics admirable, but they still make him less than perfect. This is a common flaw that we see played out in movies of all genres from *Shakespeare in Love*, to *Moulin Rouge!*, to even *A Walk to Remember.* The "wrong" guy, the troublemaking guy, the rogue from the other side of the tracks is a favorite flaw and one that works time and again.

The Playboy Flaw. This is simply a commitment phobia where the hero is afraid to settle down. We just have to take a look at the various Matthew McConaughey movies to see this played out. Try *Ghosts of Girlfriends Past*, where his is a perpetual playboy, unable to commit to the one woman who loves him. He has this same flaw in *How to Lose a Guy in 10 Days*, *Failure to Launch*, *Fool's Gold*, even *Sahara.* Mel Gibson suffers from it in *What Women Want.* It's that "I love the women, but I don't want to commit" issue. Deep inside, of course, the playboy is afraid of rejection. We all understand being afraid of rejection, so we forgive them . . . if they promise to mend their weaselly ways when they find the right woman.

The Distance Flaw. This distance can be geographical, because of age (as in time travel), social classes—anything that keeps the hero and heroine apart. This is the key flaw with Sam Baldwin in *Sleepless in Seattle.* The poor man lives half-way across the country from the heroine (not to mention that he doesn't even know her). Separation by time and/or space is a great flaw. It's often a construct of plotting, yes, but in the end, they have to confront the "distance" and do something to overcome it. We see it in movies like *The Lake House*, *Somewhere in Time*, even *You've Got Mail*, where they are separated by the Internet. Even Sam, the hero in *Ghost*, has this problem. These heroes are flawed in the fact that they are distant, and have to make the effort to bridge that gap.

There are other flaws also, such as physical limitations or broken hearts. And often, there is a deep-rooted fear behind the flaw (which we'll explore next). But give the hero a flaw and we'll want him to find a woman who can fix it!

One way to discover your hero's flaw is to ask: **Why did your last girlfriend break up with you? Or: Why haven't you found true love?**

You may be surprised at the answer!

Give your hero a fear. My husband used to hate to dance. Because he's a hero, last year he gave me dancing lessons for my birthday. Now, his fear, i.e. flaw, kept him from dancing for years because he was afraid of looking foolish, which is why we have to make sure our dancing is perfect. (It's like dancing with a drill sergeant.) I finally figured this out and helped him conquer this fear by buying us dancing tapes and helping us learn the basics in our kitchen. Then when we enrolled in dance class, he looked like he knew what he was doing. (And wow! You should see him now!)

Behind every hero's flaw there is a fear.

It's key to determine your hero's flaw. Yes, a flaw makes him less than perfect, but it also leads to a deeper issue, and the third element of a great hero: fear.

What does your hero fear? This fear must be deep—one that would keep him awake at night, or drive him to do stupid things, make stupid decisions. Sometimes a novel will start out with his fear being realized, and the result is so horrible we understand why he would run from it. A fear will build until the Black Moment until it is realized in some form. This fear—and eventually the hero's courage to face it—will cause us to love him.

Let's look at a few of the flaws we talked about earlier and see how they lead to fears.

The Sleeping Flaw *(While You Were Sleeping).* Jack can't go after the woman he loves because he doesn't want to upset the family. His fear is letting down his family. (Revealed in why he won't tell his father about his furniture business).

In *The Wedding Planner,* the hero is engaged to someone else—the wrong woman. But he is an honorable guy and he wants to see it through. His fear is breaking his promise to this girl—his college sweetheart and the woman he *should* marry. He fears letting down someone else who believes in him.

How many of us harbor the fear of disappointing someone we love? It's a legitimate fear, and one that drives a large majority of people through life. The truth behind the fear is that we may be betraying *more* people if we don't own up to the truth. Our heroes also learn it's better to live in truth and let a few people down, than live a lie.

The Troublemaker Flaw. This is Jack in *Titanic,* and Johnny in *Dirty Dancing,* and every bad boy who thinks he's not good enough for the girl. They fear that what they believe about themselves is true. They *are* trash. They aren't good enough for the girl. Of course, we, the reader, and the heroine, see the truth—they are honorable and worth loving. But having a moment where that fear comes true is a key element to helping that flaw feel insurmountable. Like Jack being arrested and handcuffed to a pipe while the Titanic sinks. And Johnny being accused of fathering a child out of wedlock. Make your troublemaker believe he *is* trouble, and his flaw will translate into a real fear.

The Playboy Flaw. The fear here is easy to diagnose. The heroes have been hurt by women in the past. Or, better yet, they've had a role model who told them that commitment will only hurt them. This fear of being hurt will keep them from enjoying life, or achieving their dreams, or even make them miserable (like their role model). In *Ghosts of Girlfriends Past,* the hero's parents loved each other, but he choked on the night he should have asked his best friend (a girl) to dance, and instead she had her first kiss with someone else. He was so hurt that he ran to his uncle, the King of the Playboys, who taught him everything he knew. This hero's fear is letting someone inside and committing to them and being hurt again.

The Distance Flaw. (*Sleepless in Seattle, The Lake House, Somewhere in Time, You've Got Mail*) This flaw can be the result of numerous fears. In *Sleepless in Seattle*, Sam Baldwin fears not finding another love like he had before. Sam Wheat, the hero in *Ghost*, fears saying the words "I love you," until it's all he has left. In *Somewhere in Time*, the hero fears travelling back to the present and losing the love in the past. When this exact thing happens, he has to confront his fear that he is from a different time than his true love is, and that perhaps their one chance is lost.

The key to finding the fear behind the flaw is looking at what they need to overcome to be with the heroine, and then tracking that back to a fear that might keep them from doing it.

Sam Baldwin (*Sleepless in Seattle*) fears uprooting his son and letting someone strange into his life just when they are starting to heal from their grief. Alex, the hero in *The Lake House*, fears waiting for time to catch up to them because the heroine might not be there when it happens. He fears losing her before he's had a chance to love her.

As your own Book Therapist, look at your character's flaw and ask: What is the fear behind the flaw? This fear will help you plot your book's tension and eventually, the moment of . . .

Make him Courageous!

Courage is the last element of a great hero. *We won't fall in love with a wimp*! A hero has to have courage to change. We don't like heroes who are stuck in their ways, who don't see their need for change, who are unwilling to take up the sword and fight the battle. A hero who is unwilling to change is a brute, a beast, and a villain.

Why is *The Matrix* so popular? Because it's about an ordinary guy who dared to reach out with his gut instincts and fight for something real and better. He can be reluctant, for sure, but in the end, he has to see the greater good of going into battle for what he wants (and ultimately, for the woman he wants).

Don't we love it, ladies, when a man is willing to do something he's never done before, for the sake of love?

Courage to change give us that delicious moment when we know that the hero or heroine are going to make it—or at least have a fighting chance.

Courage shows up when Bob, the hero in *Return to Me*, goes into the café and begs to know where Gracie is.

It's when Johnny Castle charges back into the resort and takes the stage with Baby. *(Dirty Dancing)*

When Sam reaches out on the top of the Empire State Building and takes Annie's hand. *(Sleepless in Seattle)*

When Conner Mead chases the woman he loves through the snow to tell her he loves her. *(Ghosts of Girlfriends Past)*

When Jack shows up at the subway station with a diamond ring and drops it into the change slot for Lucy. *(While You Were Sleeping)*

It even shows up in *A Walk in the Clouds*, when Paul, the hero, comes back to face the wrath of the heroine's father and asks for a second chance from her family.

Give your hero a courageous moment where he breaks through his fears, overcomes his flaws, and changes into the perfect hero that saves the day and gets the girl!

As you're plotting your story, **ask your hero: What will you do that shows your courage to change in order to get the girl?**

Give your hero these four qualities, pair him with a winning heroine, and you'll be on track to building a hero your readers will love.

Your Turn:

Take a moment to interview your Hero:

What causes are you fighting for that make us love you?

What sweet, kind, and sacrificial Boy Scout Moment will you do that make the readers love you?

Why did your last girlfriend break up with you? Or: Why haven't you found true love?

What is your flaw, and the fear behind the flaw?

What will you do that shows your courage to change in order to get the girl?

I used to hate romances. Why? Because I didn't respect a woman who had to have a man to save her. But I *did* respect a woman who allowed a man into her life to make her better, stronger, more noble, more complete.

Which is why all the heroines in my books are strong women: CIA agents, K-9 handlers, bush pilots, and fire chiefs. But for all the toughness of my heroines, they need a good man. So what makes a strong heroine?

Heroines

Give your heroine a goal. In many early romance novels, the heroine had "getting married" as her goal. This is even the goal of some heroines today, especially in historicals—Regency, Amish, Gilded Age. But if we look more closely, there is often a larger goal driving their desire to be married.

Perhaps the heroine wants to marry a duke so he can pardon her brother for a crime. Or support her sister, or child, or even rise to power to help the oppressed.

The fact is, readers have changed and the majority today want, yes, to get married and have children, but they also want something else. They want to impact their world, to be someone who does something courageous or compassionate, even bold.

In a book written for today's contemporary audience, being married is more of a *vehicle to a goal* than the goal itself. And while I'm all for marriage (and romance!) we also need to create heroines to whom readers can relate.

Thus, when you are crafting a heroine, the first element she must have is a goal. A goal gives her something proactive and causes her to fight for something she believes in. As a reader, we want to embrace her cause and fight the fight with her. Making her proactive and strong makes her noble and someone we might even want to emulate.

This goal is similar to our hero's Noble Cause. However, is our heroines are often innately noble. (It's just the way women are, let's be honest.) Not that men aren't, but most women are born nurturers, so we don't need something dark and compelling from our past in order to make us throw ourselves in front of a speeding vehicle to save our child, or sit out in the sleet to watch their football game.

But women struggle with goals. Men, on the other hand, often have no problem setting goals. It's a part of a man's innate nature.

Behind every goal is a *reason* for that goal. (And it must be a reason that resonates or makes sense to the reader.) It's in *this* way that the heroine's goal is very much like the Noble Cause of the hero.

Let's take a look at the goals of our heroines in our favorite movies:

My Big Fat Greek Wedding: Our heroine just wants to get away from her family business (the restaurant) and do her own thing. Yes, it helps that she sees the hero in the beginning, which gives her motivation, but her real goal is to respect herself and live life on her own two feet.

Shakespeare in Love: Our heroine wants to perform a role in a play—to do something for herself before she is assigned to marry a man she doesn't love.

Pride and Prejudice: Our heroine wants to marry, yes, but marry for love, not convenience. (Although she realizes that convenience is the convention of the time, and she is going against the flow.)

Return to Me: Our heroine wants to finally do the things she couldn't do when she had a bad heart: ride a bike, go to Italy, fall in love.

You've Got Mail: Our heroine wants to save her bookstore, The Shop Around the Corner. It was her mother's store and she wants to hold on to those memories.

How to Lose a Guy in 10 Days: Our heroine wants to write "meaningful" articles that can change the world.

Whatever it is, the goal must also be **measurable** and **specific**. If it isn't, how will she know if she reaches it? And it must touch the heart of your reader—something they can get behind and believe in.

A caveat here: Your heroine may not reach her goal, because along the way, she might find something better, aka the hero! But without a goal, a heroine simply isn't heroic. And she has nothing to fight for in the story.

Sometimes authors ask me if the goal of the character and the goal of the author is the same thing. *No.* Your character believes she wants/needs one thing. As the author, you will have a different goal for your character, much like a parent might have for their child. But the author goal doesn't keep your character from pushing forward to *their* goal.

Here's a hint: When you're building your romance, sometimes it helps to make a chart,(see Section 2) putting the hero on one side, the heroine on the other, and comparing and contrasting their Noble Cause and Goals. It's a great way to find those obstacles that keep them apart, which we'll talk about in a moment.

To discover your heroine's goal, ask your heroine: **What do you want?**

Give your heroine a flaw. Although your heroine has a goal, we can't let her get there, at least not without a struggle. This means our heroine also needs a flaw.

We know women aren't perfect. But we try, oh, we try. And the key to a great flaw is something that can be overcome . . . with the help of a good hero. It doesn't have to be a huge flaw. Maybe it's a tendency to run away from her problems, or better, a tendency to push men out of her life. As she gets to know the hero, he can help her overcome these flaws and grow stronger.

However, a heroine's flaw works differently than the hero's flaw. The hero's flaw is often based on his fear. I mentioned my husband's not liking to dance, which is because of his fear of looking foolish and is based on his childhood and being ridiculed.

A woman's flaw is less about her past and is more about unmet goals and things she wants to accomplish and can't or won't. It's often based on perceived fears of the future and something that *could* happen.

For example, if a woman is afraid of failure in the workplace, she might become driven, even exacting.

What if her flaw is impatience? She could be afraid that a project she is working on won't get finished, and that her coworker will steal it from her (because she is a single mother and she has to divide her time at home and the office). Maybe she doesn't trust because she thinks she can only depend on herself.

This is why flaws and fears go together. Yes, the fear *can* be based on something in the past that happened to them, but more likely it is something they've seen from others, or read, or simply believe about themselves. Whatever it is, women have a great capacity to dream up fears and then let them rule their lives. Yes, they need to be realistic, but reading about child abduction in the newspaper is enough to make a woman lock her child in the house until he's eighteen.

So, for a woman's flaw, it helps to have to look forward (while for a man's flaw looking backward is the best tool) and see if she's afraid of something that *will* happen.

Or…perhaps it is something that she wants, that she fears *won't* happen. From the moment my husband asked me to marry him to the final step down the aisle, I thought something terrible might happen to him. I feared losing him. So I became clingy and obsessed and downright scary. And he still married me!

Let's look at some heroine flaws:

In *Return to Me*, Grace, the heroine, won't let the hero kiss her because she is afraid he'll see her scar and think she's not beautiful.

In *How to Lose a Guy in 10 Days*, Andie, the heroine, won't let herself love because she is afraid that the hero will let her down (and look what falling in love did to her roommate!).

In *While You Were Sleeping*, Lucy, the heroine, won't tell the truth because she knows the family will reject her.

In a great romance, the hero figures out the woman's fear by seeing her flaws. Maybe he pries it out of her, maybe he just knows her enough to realize the truth. And, as he figures it out, he begins to address it. His job is to make her feel safe. See, a woman also wants to be protected, even if she doesn't admit it. So, as your hero becomes more heroic, the woman will release her fears.

And overcome her flaws.

As you're creating your heroine, ask: **What is your biggest flaw?**

Then ask: **Why? What fear drives this flaw**?

It's this fear that will create sympathy in your reader and perhaps even make the reader see herself in your heroine and overcome her own fears.

Note: You can weave together the fears of both the hero and the heroine and cause an event that triggers both their fears. For example, a woman might be afraid that her man will leave her, and a hero might fear that a woman will reject him or won't follow him. So, having something happen where he leaves her and she doesn't follow him is one way to trigger both fears. I always look at their fears separately, and then try and find one moment where they could come true simultaneously. Like, when a woman fears for a man's safety, so she leaves him so he won't be injured. However, he's afraid that if she needs him, he won't be there. Therefore, they're both trying to help each other, which leads to some fabulous internal obstacles!

If you're building a Hero/Heroine Chart, write in your hero's and heroine's flaws and the fears behind them. These fears can assist you in building those inner obstacles.

Give your heroine confidence. Just like we don't like wimpy heroes, we don't like flimsy heroines. It's easy for a heroine to have flaws, mostly because, if you are female author, we write about ourselves, and we all have flaws. So you need to work at putting confidence into your heroine, giving her something she's good at, that makes us applaud her.

A woman should have something we call the "**Super Power**." Something that gives her strength to stand alone, if need be. We want her to be able to turn down the rich suitor she doesn't love. Or sing "You're so vain!" to the boy who hurt her—and then walk away from him. Or go to Italy by herself. Or break up with the fiancé she doesn't love to take a chance on the one who might be waiting for her on the top of the Empire State Building.

We want to see her have confidence and believe in herself. Often, that confidence, or Super Power, rises in the end to allow her to do something that she has never done before. (Not unlike the courage we see in our hero.) However, we need to see hints of her confidence as the story progresses and as we get to know her better.

For example, Jane, the heroine in *27 Dresses*, is excellent at helping someone plan their wedding, making sure they have the perfect day. After all, she's done it at least twenty-seven times! But she is terrible at voicing her own needs, which is why she ends up in twenty-seven ugly dresses. She's also terrible at going after the man she longs for, as seen by the way her sister takes the man Jane's always loved. Our heroine even agrees to be in the wedding! Finally, the heroine is able to recognize the man she *truly* loves and, in her final Super Power moment, she goes after him, speaking up in front of a crowd of people.

Melanie, the heroine in *Sweet Home Alabama*, is excellent at controlling a staff of people and her own destiny in the designer world of New York City. But she can't seem to control anyone down in Alabama and, of course, her ex-husband is in control of her destiny. Melanie finally takes control of her heart at the end by choosing the man she's always loved.

The heroine in *Pearl Harbor* is a nurse. Evelyn can save lives and keep her cool in times of darkness. But she can't seem to heal her heart. However, she knows what the right thing to do is when she becomes pregnant. She'll "save the life" of the baby she carries—and heal herself by loving the father "with her whole heart." And in the end, Evelyn's free to love her true love without guilt.

In *Legally Blonde*, the heroine is a blonde sorority girl who flirts her way into Harvard law school. However, Elle learns that she can be a fabulous lawyer if she wants it, and success has nothing to do with her hair color and everything to do with her abilities. However, it is her sorority girl skills that help her solve the case that no one else can. And, in the end, Elle tells off the man who broke her heart and goes it alone.

Give your heroine some confidence: something she does well and something she then uses to stand up and become truly heroic in her darkest moment.

When you're building your heroine, ask: **What are you good at and how does that Super Power help save the day?**

Combine that question with asking your heroine: **What can you do at the end of the book that you couldn't do at the beginning?**

Now you have the makings of a heroic heroine.

On your chart, fill in your hero's courageous moment and your heroine's confident moment and you'll be generating ideas for the Sacrificial/Big Gesture scene!

Give your heroine a unique beauty. Once you've created a heroine with a super power, despite her flaws and fears, one who has a goal that will drive her through the story, you have one last element of a heroic heroine.

What is beauty? An informal Warren family poll taken a couple years ago elicited very different responses:

16-year-old boy: Someone who is smart.
13-year-old boy: A girl who can run fast. (This answer only recently became clear when he fell for a cute sprinter in track.)
11-year-old boy: Nice hair.
15-year-old girl: Someone who is unique.
Married old guy: Softness. Someone who is happy and cheerful.

What makes someone beautiful? I think we can all agree that beauty comes from inside. A crabby person, regardless of how beautiful, gives off an ugly sheen. But an unattractive person who exudes kindness can be very pretty.

When we're creating a heroine, especially in a romance, she has to possess her own beauty. Something special and unique, hers alone, and something only the hero can see and love. Maybe it's her eyes, but also the way she can look right through him and see what he needs. Or maybe it's her patience. Maybe it's her strength to see the good, or believe in the good. Whatever it is, the hero sees it like no one else can. The heroine might be genuinely pretty—and then gets even prettier as the hero gets to know her. Or, she could be plain and turns gorgeous as her inner nature is revealed. The key is, the hero has to see her beauty and appreciate it.

Consider one of my favorite actresses, Jodie Foster. Love her. She's an amazing actress. And while she's pretty, I wouldn't peg her as crazy-beautiful. One of my favorite movies of hers is *Maverick*, where she stars as a gambler against Mel Gibson. She's a scamp, (and he likewise), doing whatever is necessary to get into the big poker tournament (even stealing Mel's money!) But the more she tricks Mel and teases him, the more she turns irresistible to him. Her scoundrel ways are what draws him to her, and they make a perfect team.

The hero has to not only see the heroine's special beauty, but also communicate it -- either to her or someone else in the story.

While You Were Sleeping has a great scene with this element. Jack wants to play cards with his brother Peter, who is still in a coma, and Jack says, "The winner gets Lucy." Love that scene!

Or what about in *How to Lose a Guy in 10 Days* when the hero tells his friends why this woman drives him crazy?

Even in *Sleepless in Seattle*, Sam Baldwin tells his friends about this woman he saw at the airport. He noticed *her* out of all the other people in the airport.

When you're looking for the unique beauty of your heroine, ask: **What is beautiful about your heroine that only (or especially) your hero can see?**

Or perhaps your hero needs more help.

What makes a heroine beautiful?

Beauty is unique to every man, every person. I see beauty in my daughter's creativity, her independent spirit. My husband sees his daughter's cheerful smile, the way she admires him. I don't know what the boys in her class see (maybe I don't want to know), but I know her friends see someone who listens, who gives wise advice.

It's these inner qualities that make a heroine beautiful (and likewise, makes a man handsome!) However, they are specific to each person. So, what does your hero see in your heroine? How do we discover your heroine's unique beauty?

We start "with the eye of the beholder" and we look at their vacancies and their strengths.

1. What are your beholder's vacancies?

   Everyone has things they are *not* good at. Maybe it's the tendency to speak when you should listen. Maybe it's being wound so tight you can't relax. Maybe it's the inability to commit to something, for fear of it backfiring. Whatever it is, we are often drawn to someone who has a strength in that area. I'm hearing Jerry Maguire (movie of the same name) in my head saying, "You . . . complete me." **It's those opposite, completing qualities that a hero might find attractive,** as well as sometimes annoying! My sweet hubby can be brusque and insensitive sometimes. He counts on me to be the gentle one, to clue him into his foibles.

   Ask: How does your heroine complement or balance the hero?

2. What are your beholder's strengths?

   My husband is an adventurer. He loves to travel and discover new things. And he loves the fact that I am a willing participant. Not only that, I hand over my visa and the map and say, "Wherever we end up, I trust you." (This has taken some training over the years!) But I've heard him say, "I love the fact that you keep up with me." Beauty is also found in acceptance, encouragement, and like-mindedness. **A man loves a woman who loves the things he loves.**

   Ask: What does your heroine do that affirms the hero? How does she accentuate his strengths?

As the story progresses, your hero will see the outside of your heroine less and less, and her inside more and more, which will only accentuate her beauty on the outside. If she has freckles and lots of wild hair that at first is off-putting, he might gradually see her laughter and acceptance of him, and begin to love how they reveal her personality, until he adores those freckles and wild hair.

(This doesn't just apply to heroes, either. It can be a mother-daughter relationship or a friend-to-friend relationship. We all have vacancies and strengths, and people in our lives complement our vacancies or accentuate our strengths.)

The fulfillment of the hero's vacancies and the accentuation of his strengths combine to make your heroine irresistible.

3. Irresistibility is the final element of beauty—it's that package of all these elements that makes a woman (or man) simply take over our hearts.

How does irresistibility work? Consider *Return to Me.* Why is the heroine irresistible to the hero? First, because Bob's desperately lonely. Grace fills that vacancy through her embrace of others. She has a wide "family," while he's a loner, and has a hard time caring even for himself. The scene where Bob's dog eats from the kitchen drawer is hilarious as well as sad. Grace also adds to his strengths. She has a sense of humor he finds endearing. (Remember the bottled water scene?) Grace's humor and strength encourages Bob's ebbing spirit to keep going. (Remember, he's building a gorilla park, against all odds).

My favorite line is after Grace has left, and Bob goes in to talk with the old guys, asking for her address. He doesn't know what to do and says, "I ache for Gracie." She has a place inside him, and missing her has left a giant hole. Wonderful! Irresistible!

Maybe it's simply easier to ask your hero, **What draws you to her? Why can't you live without her?**

If this feels too cumbersome, simply ask: How is your heroine irresistible to you?

Make the heroine beautiful to the hero and she'll be beautiful to the reader.

Your Turn:

Interview your heroine:

What do you want?

What is your biggest flaw?

Why? What fear drives this flaw?

What are you good at and how does that Super Power help save the day?

What can you do at the end of the book that you couldn't do at the beginning?

What is beautiful about your heroine that only (or especially) your hero can see?

How does your heroine complement or balance the hero?

What does your heroine do that affirms the hero?

How does she accentuate his strengths?

Ask the Hero:
What draws you to her? Why can't you live without her?

How is your heroine irresistible to you?

INGREDIENT 2: INTEREST/NEED

"Of all the gin joints, in all the towns, in all the world, she walks into mine."
~Rick Blaine (played by Humphrey Bogart) in Casablanca

We'll touch on why fools fall in love in a moment, but before you can start your romance, you need to get them together on the page.

Which means they need to meet.

In a romance, the Inciting Incident is often the meeting of the hero and heroine. It's that moment where they walk into each other's lives and everything changes. It is possible to have an Inciting Incident separate from the meeting of the hero and heroine, as long as the Inciting Incident *leads* to their meeting.

And, in a romance, this meeting has to happen by chapter three. In a category romance, or a novel of less than 75K, this meeting should generally happen in chapter one, and preferably in the first few pages.

There are two components necessary to this moment when your hero and heroine meet: Interest and Need.

1. Build Interest. In other words, make something about the other person stand out.

For example, in *Sleepless in Seattle*, it's the voice of the heroine's son and his sad situation that captures Annie's attention.

In *While You Were Sleeping*, it's the fact that Lucy, Peter's supposed fiancée, is staying the night on the sofa. Jack has never heard of her before and they meet when he interrupts her sneaking out of his parents' home.

In *A Walk in the Clouds*, Paul is selling chocolates after the war (and after he and his wife are estranged) and meets Victoria crying on a bus. She's beautiful and he can't resist listening to her story and wanting to help.

In *Return to Me*, the hero and heroine meet while he's on a blind date with another woman. He sees Grace, who is a waitress, filling up a bottle of water with tap water for his high-maintenance date. He keeps her secret and is rewarded with a take-out dinner when he makes excuses to leave early. Thankfully, he's left his cell phone behind in the restaurant, which nets him a date with Grace when he goes to pick it up.

The key to this moment is something that stands out about the hero and heroine to each other. They've created Interest.

Here are some ways I've had my hero and heroine meet:

In my book, *Nothing But Trouble,* PJ Sugar meets her love interest, Jeremy, when she breaks into the house of a deceased friend. Jeremy is a private investigator (PI), posing as a pizza delivery man, also breaking into the house to search for clues. They escape together and the romance sparks.

In *Happily Ever After*, my heroine, Mona, puts out an ad for a handyman—and Joe walks into her house in his muddy boots, looking for a job.

In *The Perfect Match*, my heroine, Ellie, is the fire chief and she saves the life of the hero, Dan.

In *Nightingale*, my heroine meets the hero through a letter mistakenly sent to her. It comes at a time of grief and his kind words make an impact on her.

In *Escape to Morning*, my hero nearly runs over my heroine's K-9 dog.

However your hero and heroine meet, it must make an impact, stand out, create interest for the hero and heroine . . . and the reader. We want to notice them to notice each other!

Ask: What about this meeting and this person, stands out? What stirs the interest of the point of view (POV) character?

2. It's not just an interesting person or situation that creates this ingredient. We all meet interesting people every day. Why this day, this moment? **It's because they are at a place of Need in their life.**

The hero or heroine is ready for love. Perhaps they don't even know it, but the author has created a situation that has their heart longing for love. It doesn't mean they aren't resistant to it, or that they won't fight it, but deep inside something about them feels empty. And only the hero/heroine can fill that emptiness.

In *Sleepless in Seattle*, Sam longs for—but doesn't believe he will ever find—that perfect woman.

Annie, too, is looking for that romance that feels perfect. She's even asked her mother if she's marrying the right man. Even though she's in a relationship, it doesn't fulfill her like the dream of finding the love that Sam talked about on the radio.

In *While You Were Sleeping*, Jack expresses jealousy that Peter always succeeds. "It's not fair," Jack says. Just once, he'd like to get the girl.

Lucy is desperately lonely and lives to see Peter walk by her subway stand each day. She is willing to marry him because she has nothing else. (Until she has Jack and realizes she can't marry someone she doesn't love.)

In *A Walk in the Clouds*, Paul has returned from war, hoping his wife has missed him even though she never wrote to him. His heart is broken when she practically throws him out.

Victoria has found a man who is honest and honorable and won't use her, like her college professor did.

In *Return to Me*, Bob isn't sure he's ready to date again after the death of his wife, even though his friends say he is. But his life is lonely and his heart is healed enough to try.

Grace wants to live for the first time in her life. As her father said to Bob, "When she met you, her heart beat truly for the first time."

Why this guy? Why this gal? Why are your hero and heroine ready for love?

Ask your hero and heroine: Why would you like to fall in love? You'll find your answer. More than that, knowing this answer will assist you in crafting that moment when all their wounds are healed and they're able to fully give away their hearts.

Ask the Hero: What about this meeting and this person, stands out? What stirs your interest?

Ask the Heroine: What about this meeting and this person, stands out? What stirs your interest?

Ask the Hero: Why would you like to fall in love?

Ask the Heroine: Why would you like to fall in love?

INGREDIENT 3: WHY

Why do fools fall in love? I could list off all the reasons why I love my husband: He's kind, and he believes in me, and he's patient when I'm not, and he's wise. Yes, these are all great attributes, but they aren't necessarily the reason I fell in love with him. I remember our first date. We sat on the beach and chatted until 2 a.m. (No kissing at all!) And what did we talk about? Our values—the things that were important to us—and the biggest of those was our desire to be missionaries.

The glue that draws two people together isn't that they both like tennis, or the same television shows—it's that their values have connected deep inside.

I love to teach, and one of my favorite events is the annual MBT Deep Thinker's Retreat. I get together with twenty or so other authors and assist them in crafting their stories. I love it for three big reasons.

First, I live in the woods, and when I say woods, I mean tucked into a little hamlet in the snowy tip of northern Minnesota, where ice and snow clasp us in solitude for the better part of four months. Worse, I am an extrovert, so . . . well, you get the picture. I shed my layers going south, meet my friends, stand on the beach, and shout out a hallelujah! The retreat *fills that empty place*. You could say it *completes me*.

Secondly, I get to do what I love: teach about writing craft. The writers need to learn brings out the *best* in me.

Lastly, these writers are there because they have a desire to write amazing stories. Theire values touch the heart of my Core Values.

Earlier, we talked about beauty, and we looked at it from the hero's POV, or "the eye of the beholder." We asked the hero to look at the heroine based on his vacancies, as well as his strengths.

But this applies to the heroine too and helps us unlock the mystery of true love. Let's take a broader look and apply it to our hero and our heroine.

Why do people fall in love?

1. **A hero and heroine complete each other.**

   We are drawn to people who "complete" us—who can do the things we can't do. I am what I call a "fire-starter." I have lots of great ideas. My husband knows how to complete them. Thankfully, we get a lot done this way.

   This can be a difficult element to define in a book. What can the hero do for the heroine that she can't? And vice-versa?

   In *Sleepless in Seattle*, Annie can travel to Seattle whereas Sam can't leave his home to find her.

   In *While you Were Sleeping*, Jack can give Lucy the world (or at least a stamp in her passport).

   In *A Walk in the Clouds,* Victoria gives Paul a family. He gives her respectability.

Ask: What can your hero and heroine do for each other that they can't do themselves? Then, have them do it.

2. **They hero and heroine make each other better people.**

   We like people who can see the best in us and draw it out. I'm a very impatient person. My husband, however, is patient and encourages me to wait. My husband is very black and white, I help him see the gray areas. We are better together.

   In *Sleepless in Seattle*, Annie believes in romance and Happily Ever After. It's her belief in this one true love that propels her to the top of the Empire State Building and into Sam's arms. And, she's stirred in him a hope of something new and right, also.

   In *While you Were Sleeping*, Lucy convinces Jack to tell his father the truth about his love for furniture making.

   In *A Walk in the Clouds*, Victoria draws Paul into her world and helps him heal and become a part of a heritage.

Ask: What does your heroine do that affirms the hero? That accentuates his strengths? (And vice versa.) How do they become better people when they are together?

4. **The hero and heroine share essential values.**

We like people who understand and embrace what we believe in, who hold our values dear to their hearts. It's more than goals or a similar life plan—because those can change. It's that core belief deep inside. Call it a vision statement, maybe, but it's that core statement about life, faith, and purpose that glues people together.

Christians like to marry Christians, Jews like to marry Jews, and Muslims like to marry fellow Muslims. Why? Because each of these religions come with a set of values and beliefs that translate into expected behaviors. This is why it's difficult to marry outside your faith. Even within denominations it can be difficult. Catholics marry Catholics, Lutherans marry Lutherans and Baptists marry Baptists. When two opposite worlds collide, it can be confusing.

When we don't share core values, then we run into trouble, and not just with religion. Raising children, handling finances, dealing with in-laws, and the list goes on. Is it possible to have the same core values without having the same religion? Absolutely. The bottom line is, couples who believe in something together, i.e. true love, or that God is in control, or even that they will protect their children at all costs, that freedom is worth fighting for forge an unbreakable bond. My husband and I share the belief that our lives are in God's hands, and we can trust him. And that without grace we'd be lost. Whatever challenges we encounter, we connect on a core level that strengthen us. In essence, we *get* or understand each other.

Even people who are vastly different may agree at their core that their *differences* are their strength. That their belief in the essential value of others binds them together.

Just a note here: Your characters' core values may change during the course of the story, but at the end, they find that common ground.

Annie and Sam bond over the belief in true love. (*Sleepless in Seattle*)
Jack and Lucy share the value of family. (*While You Were Sleeping*)
Victoria and Paul value heritage and honor. (*A Walk in the Clouds*)
And Rick and Ilsa (*Casablanca*) believe in freedom.

When you are developing your character, you will naturally discover their core values. We'll explore how to get at the root of this when we explore the Backstory, and the **Dark Moment**. But for now . . .

Ask: What core values do the hero and heroine share? How can you reveal them to the reader, and to each other?

Why do fools fall in love? I don't think we even know ourselves when we are in the middle of it. But when the dust clears, well, hopefully it's because you complete each other, you're better together, and you understand each other.

When you are writing a romance, writing these three elements into the story will convince your reader that indeed, these fools have fallen in love!

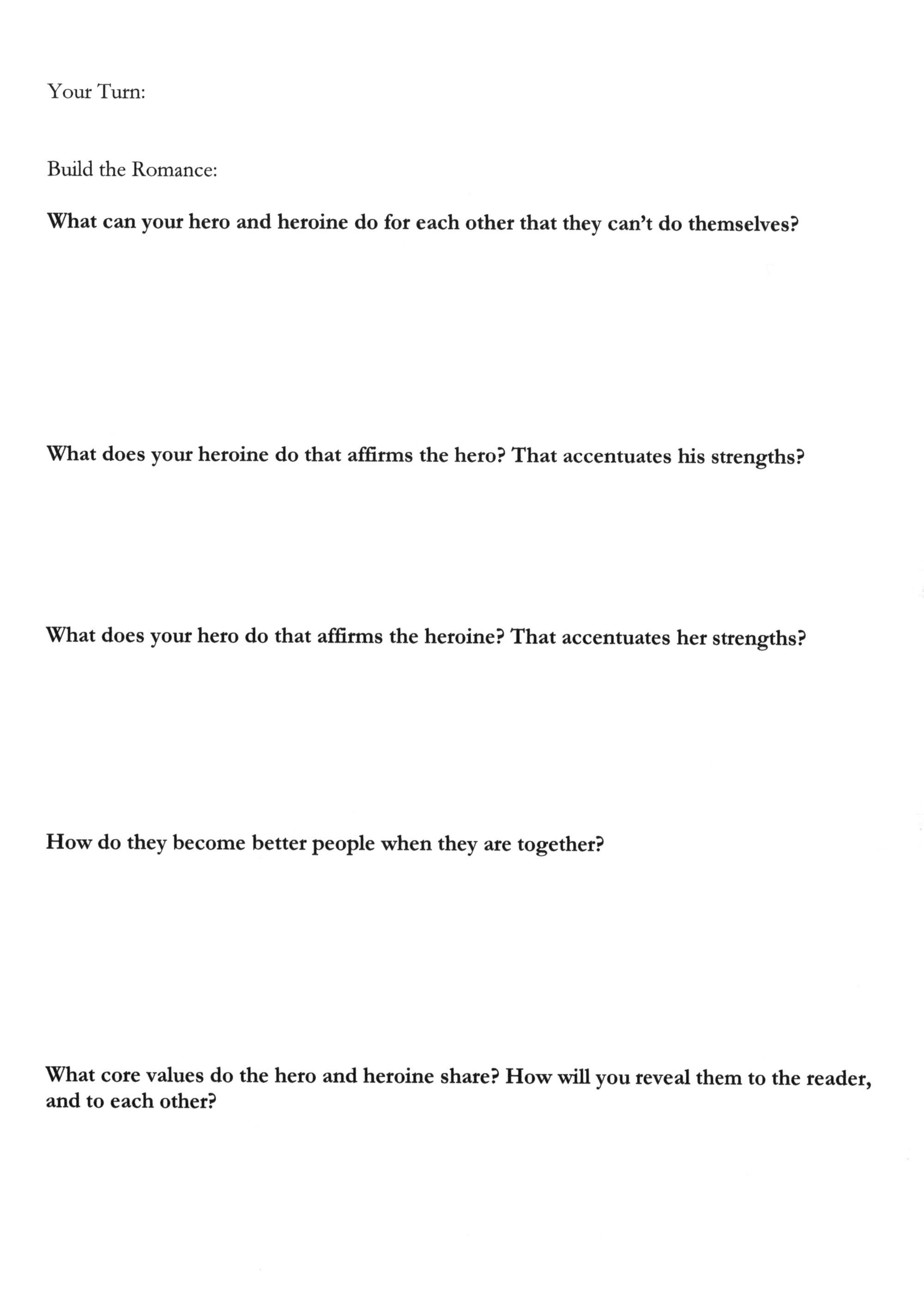

Your Turn:

Build the Romance:

What can your hero and heroine do for each other that they can't do themselves?

What does your heroine do that affirms the hero? That accentuates his strengths?

What does your hero do that affirms the heroine? That accentuates her strengths?

How do they become better people when they are together?

What core values do the hero and heroine share? How will you reveal them to the reader, and to each other?

INGREDIENT 4: WHY NOT?

But what about the tension? So far, we've just had all the reasons the hero and heroine should fall in love. But a great book is also about why they can't fall in love (and do anyway). Which means you need what I call the "Why Nots."

Falling in love is amazing. Regardless of your age, when you find that one you love, it stirs a breathlessness, an awakening in us that our beloved would, well, *love us*. Because, frankly, we know ourselves enough to know that they shouldn't. Right? We think: If he or she only knew the truth, they'd go running.

But, eventually they do find out the truth, and they stay. And that's what makes true love even more breathtaking.

Add to that the little sacrifices we make for the ones we love, and pretty soon, life is a romance novel!

But the fact is, without a few struggles, true love isn't tested. Remember your first big fight? I'll bet you bemoaned with your friends and said, "That's it. It's over."

Which made it ever more wonderful when the one you loved showed up at the door at 1 a.m., red-eyed . . .

A romance novel is the delicate balance of conflict and desire. There must be enough desire (Why) to create interest and stir need. But, *conflict* drives the story. Without the fights and the turmoil, the story isn't interesting. It's just sappy. Most of all, how can True Love triumph if it doesn't have to? Is it true love if it isn't tested? We're not sure, which means that conflict is essential for a great romance. But not just any conflict, like fighting over the kind of coffee they drink, or driving too fast, or even stupider things like fighting about the way he or she did or did not look at our character from across the office. This kind of conflict is trite and unsatisfying.

No, your hero and heroine are going to fight about the things that *matter*.

In other words, our conflict is going to be focused on the true obstacles to love between them. Something that I like to call the **Why Nots.**

A romance novel must have both External Why Nots and Internal Why Nots.

External Why Nots

The external Why Nots should be easy: Why can't these two people be together? Think of the external obstacles as the plot obstacles:

- ✓ He works for the bank that wants to take over the family farm.
- ✓ She is his new boss, and is supposed to fire him.
- ✓ He opens a competing business in her town.
- ✓ She's a cop, he's a criminal.
- ✓ He's a bounty hunter, assigned to track down his ex-wife.

External Obstacles usually arise from competing Goals and Noble Causes. They are equally valid, equally strong, and equally compelling. And thus, big enough to keep your hero and heroine apart.

Let's take a look at the obstacles in our favorite movies:

***While You Were Sleeping*:** She's his brother's fiancée. Or not, but then yes, she is. So, he can't have her. And, she has lied and can't get out of it. These obstacles loom larger as the story plays out. (This theme is used *a lot* in movies, by the way, and it never seems to get old. Think: *Sabrina*. Or, even *Maid of Honor*. The device of belonging to the wrong person and loving the right one is popular and effective.)

***Return to Me*:** She has his dead wife's heart. 'Nuf said.

***Casablanca*:** Well, Ilsa is married, isn't she? And it's clear that two people's problems don't amount to a hill of beans in this crazy world. More than that, her husband is a real hero, a great guy, and Rick is a man who believes in freedom enough to let her go for a greater cause.

Note: The external Why Not can also be derived by something internal, but it emerges in something physical. For example, in my novel *Happily Ever After*, my hero has a brother who has Down Syndrome. This is an external obstacle only because it caused an internal obstacle: The hero's father left his mother when he couldn't deal with the stress of the brother's medical condition. The hero's wounded past created internal obstacles that manifest in the external obstacle of having a brother with special needs.

External Obstacles are sometimes difficult to pinpoint and not be cliché. How many times can an author do the "wrong side of the tracks" variant? Amish versus Englisher, high society versus working class, North versus South, etc? But the very fact that we have so many of these situations proves that this obstacle is very real.

Turn the obstacle over and look at it creatively. How can you put a new twist on the obstacles?

Here are some recent ones I've used:

- ✓ She's an American writing to a German prisoner of war (POW) in Wisconsin. (A variant of the "wrong side of the tracks.")
- ✓ He's supposed to be her bodyguard. (The work related obstacle.)
- ✓ She suspects him of sabotaging her business.(Intrigue-related)
- ✓ He destroyed her hotel, and she wants money from him. (Opposing financial goals)
- ✓ She is trying to prove that he committed a crime. (Intrigue-related)
- ✓ She slept with his brother!
- ✓ She's the fire chief, he's on her crew. (Work-related)
- ✓ He's a Russian FSB agent, she's an American missionary on the lam. (Intrigue-related)
- ✓ She's a private eye (PI), he's a cop who is trying to get her to fail. (Opposing relationship goals)
- ✓ And, numerous times I've used, "He or she broke her or his heart." (It works.)

The External Obstacles are the key to creating tension in your story. Without them, the reader will say, "Grow up already and fall in love!"

Ask: What realistic External Obstacle in the plot pushes your hero and heroine apart?

Make them realistic, and you'll have a powerful reason why they can't be together.

Internal Why Nots

Although we've discovered the plot or external obstacles (the Why Nots) that keep our characters apart, we're not finished causing problems. Remember, the point of a great romance is for love to overcome the obstacles and triumph! Which means we must have Internal Obstacles, or the reasons why we (and our characters) run from love.

Finding internal obstacles isn't difficult. We can all come up with a long list of the reasons why we are unlovable. Our sins, our flaws, or fears, our idiosyncrasies —you name it. It's a wonder we don't all live as hermits!

The problem with finding internal obstacles is finding the right ones. Often authors either pick too many or focus *only* on the internals as the obstacles to love. This causes your story to end up being circular and boring as the hero and heroine rehash their issues over and over.

We also pick *too many* obstacles (because they are so easy to pick! We just climb inside the skin of our character and ask "Why won't she love you?" Let the bemoaning begin!)

How do we solve these problems?

Just pick one. One Big Why Not. One Big Why Not that has many facets. One Big Why Not that has many facets that is built off of a wound in your character's past. One wound, from one event. One event that they can then share with the heroine or hero when the time is right.

See, our internal obstacles to love are usually based off some event that caused us great pain. It could be an old romance, or it could be something done or said to us as a child. It could be a failure in the teenage years, or even something that happened to someone close to us. Whatever that wound was, it causes us to shy away from love and not be willing to risk it. It is also an excellent tool for plotting in the internal obstacles.

Here are some possible woundings that might create internal Why Nots:

- ✓ "I am afraid of love because my mother left me on my aunt's doorstep when I was six. I still remember her driving away. Thus, I am afraid of abandonment."

- ✓ "I drove drunk when I was seventeen, and got into an accident that killed my high school sweetheart. I'm afraid to love because I hurt everyone I love."

- ✓ "The man I loved got me pregnant and left me the sophomore year of college. I am afraid of loving because I know I'll be rejected and left with the pieces of my future."

If you create an event in your character's past, something that leaves a deep wound, then your character will do anything not to be wounded in this way again, and thus, will walk around trying to protect himself. Including turning his back on True Love if he thinks he'll get hurt.

Ask your character: What is the worst thing that ever happened to you (preferably romantically, but it can be anything that involves the heart) and what wound did it leave?

It helps if this is an actual event, something they can tell the heroine (or hero) later. I often see people use general events – e.g. my character comes from a broken home, so he's afraid of love. That's a starting place, but I always push them to find a singular event inside that overall situation that epitomizes their wound. It must also be compelling enough to create a wound in the first place. This event is used to create a heartbreaking and poignant scene when they share it with the one they love. And becomes a moment of triumph when they are loved, anyway!

To Why or Why Not: Exploring the Romance Story Arcs

So, why do Why and Why Nots matter? It's not just about creating tension. Why and Why Nots help you craft the Story Arc.

Is your romance a Why/Why Not? Or a Why Not/Why?

There are two basic structures, or story arcs, to a romance—whether it's a straight up romance, or just a romance thread. This structure helps you to know where to insert the different components of your romance.

The first structure is **Why/Why Not:**

These are stories that have our characters falling in love in the beginning, with no major obstacles in their way, only to discover obstacles half-way or even later. It's not about how we as the reader see their journey, but **how the characters see it**.

***Return to Me*:** The hero and heroine meet and instantly hit it off. They have a similar sense of humor, and they like similar foods and have fun together, even have some romantic sparks. *Until* she discovers she has her boyfriend's deceased wife's heart. Suddenly we've arrive at the Why Not part of the story.

***You've Got Mail*:** The hero and heroine love each other online, have similar interests, similar love of New York and books and business drive. They are perfect for each other *until* they find out they are enemies in real life. Enter, the Why Not.

Let's look at the other structure: the **Why Not/Why** stories.

In a Why Not/Why story structure, the external and internal obstacles (Why Nots) keep them apart even as the Why pulls them together. Then, when it seems that the Why will win the day, the biggest Why Not rises to break them apart.

***Sleepless in Seattle*:** The hero and heroine have so much Why Not in front of them, it seems they'll never get to the Why. Again, it's in the viewpoint of the character, not the reader, because from the beginning we can see that these two belong together. Why Not: She's engaged to someone else, they live thousands of miles apart, she doesn't even know him, he thinks she's loony (or at least among the strange women writing to him). It's not until the end that they realize they belong together and discover the Why.

***While You were Sleeping*:** The Why Nots are glaring: He's her, um, fiancés, brother. And of course, she's lying, but that only adds to the Why Not, until she's revealed as a liar. But by then, they've seen the Whys and that is what causes the angst.

As you're beginning to plot your romance—even before you nail down the component elements—think through the structure of your story. Do you have the Why first and then the big Why Not? Or is the Why Not glaring, until finally the Why is too big to ignore?

In the early stages of my plotting, I start with creating the hero and heroine. Then I assemble a few of the key ingredients: why they belong together, why not, what their sparks are, their happily ever after. Nothing is written in stone, however.

Then, to get going, I nail down the story arc: Why/Why Not or Why Not/Why. Knowing what kind of story arc I'll have helps me to know where to drop in the components. For example, if I'm building a Why/Why Not story, I'll have the interest, the wooing and Why element, as well as the kiss, and perhaps even a glimpse of the happily ever after at the beginning. (They need to know what they have to live for!) Then, I'll throw in the Why Not, with lots of sparks and the Black Moment.

If I have a Why Not Structure, then I'll start with sparks, a touch of interest, perhaps a hint of wooing, all the while keeping the Why Nots paramount, gradually leading up to the kiss, before we get to the big sacrifice and the Why.

These structures and the flow of the elements will become clearer as we explore the remaining ingredients. Later, you'll learn how to plug in the different elements into your three act structure, and how to craft both kinds of stories, but for now, take a look at your romance structure. **Is it a Why/Why Not, or a Why Not/Why?**

Your Turn:

What realistic External Obstacles in the plot push your hero and heroine apart?

Ask your hero: What is the worst thing that ever happened to you (preferably romantically, but it can be anything that involves the heart) and what wound did it leave?

Ask your heroine: What is the worst thing that ever happened to you and what wound did it leave?

Is your story a Why/Why Not, or a Why Not/Why? Sketch it out for your own understanding.

INGREDIENT 5: WOOING (DATING YOUR READER!)

In every romance the key is making your characters fall in love, right? We've talked about *how* we fall in love--how we connect to each other's core values, and how we complement each other and make each other into stronger people.

However, how do you write that journey, step by step? How do you woo your reader into falling in love with your characters too? You have to date your reader.

Remember the last time you fell in love? You saw him or her across the room, and something about their physical appearance intrigued you. It told you something about them. Perhaps they were brave, or strong, or creative, or disheveled, or rough-edged. You probably noticed their mannerisms, maybe how they talked, how they smiled, how they handled themselves. Even before you met, their clothing and demeanor gave you a general impression about them.

Then you met them. You found out their name, where they were from. You saw how they treated the waitress, or the hotel clerk, or an employee. Perhaps you saw their habits, their music, their tastes in décor, their car. Hopefully, you also saw how they reacted to situations of joy or stress. This gave you a hint about their internal character, what they were good at, even hinted at their values.

After a first date, you might have discovered their life goals and maybe what he or she wants most. You may have talked about your childhood, or your dreams and what struggles you face finding them. You may have gotten a glimpse at a major event that shaped their life. All of this revealed their purpose in life, the **Noble Cause** that drove them to make the choices they made.

Perhaps after a few dates, you had a first fight. He or she reacted to that fear of getting hurt. In that moment, you saw their history with love, maybe even a hint at their deepest fears, making you think back to the events that shaped them. Suddenly, you felt as if you looked inside their heart. If your fight made you a stronger couple, then it made your heart more tender toward him or her as you understood their insecurities and embraced their dreams.

Finally, you came to the place where you knew you had to go forward or break up. You came to that barrier between dating and true love, and if they struggled to cross it, you saw their darkest fears and the wound, maybe even a belief that kept him or her from finding happiness.

Hopefully he or she broke through the barrier with an Epiphany or Truth that gave them the courage to declare their love.

Ahh . . . I love seeing the heart of someone else and embracing it. This is how you fall in love. And how your reader will too. *The key to wooing your reader is a technique called* ***Character Layering*.**

Character Layering

Character Layering is all about slowly revealing the heart of your character—to your other characters in the story and, ultimately, to your reader.

But doesn't your reader need to know about your character in order to love him? No.

I hear this often from people who might pour everything—all the great reasons why our hero and heroine are the way they are, their history, their hurts, their triumphs—onto the first page. Think back: If you knew everything about your spouse or significant other when you met them, would you still go forward? Perhaps it's best if we fall in love layer by layer.

More than that, your reader wants to dive into the story. Too much too soon just bogs the story down. If you dump your hero's entire bio onto the first page, not only will it seem forced, but it also will lack impact. The fun of getting to know a character is discovering who they are and what makes them tick. The best part of a book is discovering the **Dark Past,** or desperate motivation, behind their actions. If you reveal it all at once it lacks punch, and you've stolen the emotional impact of the story from the reader.

Character Layering solves the problem of what to tell, when.

The reason we see huge chunks of **Backstory** in a novel is because the author is trying to figure out their own character. They're getting into their character's skin and working through his layers to figure out his behavior. This is perfectly acceptable . . . for a rough draft. Go ahead and take as many pages as you need and then cut out the backstory. Put it in a "Character" file and *then* start your story.

But I'm getting ahead of myself. Before you can unlayer your character, or even start your story, you have to build your character. And that means Backstory.

Building a Character's Backstory

It is essential to know the Backstory of your character *before* you start the book. Why? As I mentioned, you want to start your story quickly, without too much bio. But you need to understand your character because it's their Backstory that causes them to react in the here and now. The reader just needs to see the *outcome* of the Backstory and how it affected your character.

So, how much Backstory should you develop?

Answer: Enough to know your characters motivations for why he or she does the things they do in your story.

If your character loved to draw as a child and always dreamed of being an artist, that's only important if it has something to do with the plot. If he's a detective solving a murder, it might not have anything to do with the story. However, if he is asked to draw the suspect and rediscovers the rusty talent he had, then perhaps it is slightly important. Even better, if he loved to draw, and had talent, but his father told him he was a terrible artist (in order to discourage such a "frivolous" career), and the story is about a policeman who discovers that he has the ability to see the crimes in the pictures he draws, (and thus was always meant to use this God-given gift) well, suddenly this Backstory takes on relevance.

I've read countless books where the character seems to have been born on page one. They're flat, uninteresting, even unbelievable. Even worse, however, is when the character's entire life history is fleshed out in the first three chapters. I'm not going to remember (as a reader) what college the hero or heroine went to. But tell me that he witnessed a murder as a ten-year-old, and yes, that I'll remember.

Developing the Backstory

If you've taken any of my classes, read the My Book Therapy (MBT) blog, or read *From the Inside . . . Out*, you know I like to use the Five Elements of Self-Esteem as a foundation for plotting and character development. I also like to use them for building the elements of layering.

For a more in-depth explanation of the Five Elements of Self-Esteem and how to build them into a plot, check out *From the Inside . . . Out.* (This is available through the My Book Therapy store at www.mybooktherapy.com)

The Five Elements of Self-Esteem help us determine who our character is, why they do the things they do, what their greatest fears and dreams are, how to make them suffer, how to craft the Black Moment, their perfect Epiphany, and finally, the happily ever after ending.

The five elements will also help us layer our character, step by step.

What are the components of our character's layers?

1. **Identity:** Everyone has an identity they use to introduce themselves to others. The first layer reflects how they see themselves or how the world sees them.

When you meet someone for the first time, you are basing your impressions on who they are by how they dress, what they are doing at the time, perhaps the speech they use, and the way they introduce themselves. This gives us the first glimpse as to who they are. So, who is your character? What identity does he give himself? What external trappings go along with that identity?

What impression do they give to the world because of that identity?

For example, from my book *Happily Ever After,* my hero, Joe, considers himself a drifter. When he meets the heroine, Mona, for the first time, he looks like a drifter— he has a wreck of a truck, a duffle bag, a mangy dog, faded jeans, work boots, a flannel shirt, a scruffy beard, a hint of unkempt hair. He even wears his muddy boots into her house, indicating that he really doesn't think about things like decorum. He's showing that he's much more concerned about hard work and hiding himself than he is about presenting a clean image.

Ask: Who is your character? What sort of attire, behaviors, mannerisms, and trappings go along with their identity?

Don't panic and think *that's so stereotypical!* I don't want you to write cardboard characters. We're just setting up the components of the layers and, as you go, you'll discover even more facets to your character's identity.

2. **Noble cause/Purpose:** Behind every hero, there's a reason why he does the things he does. In *Braveheart*, the death of his bride compels William Wallace to fight for a free Scotland. In *The Bourne Identity*, it's Jason Bourne's quest to discover who he is.

In determining your character, you need to know what happened in his past that made him the person he is today. **What was his darkest moment?** Usually, it is this moment that contributes to his Noble Cause. Usually a person will do anything to make sure this dark moment is not repeated. Often the Noble Cause is directly related to either atoning for that dark moment, or protecting himself or others from it.

As we touched on earlier, the Dark Moment is best if it is one specific moment, something that you might even journal in order to pull every nuance from it. The darkest moment also creates a superb foundation for letting the hero/heroine see through his/her cracks to the vulnerable heart of the man/woman inside.

From the Dark Moment, you will also pull the Greatest Fear (which assists you in creating the Black Moment), the Wound (as we touched on earlier. The Wound is also used to create the Breakup), and even the Lie that they believe, that set of beliefs about life and/or God that determine their choices and their emotional/spiritual journey.) Take your time in developing this Dark Moment of the past. It's key to every significant element of your story, so you want it well-thought out.

You'll also use this information in developing a **Layer of Revelation. Ask: What happened in your past that molded your goals and purposes today?**

3. **Competence:** We like heroes who can take care of themselves, who know what they're doing. It builds our confidence in them and causes them to be heroic. What is that one thing that your hero does well?

The Bourne Identity is a wonderful movie that showcases Bourne's skills. We know that his girlfriend is safe with him, even though many assassins are on their tail.

Even computer geeks can be heroic when we see them using their skills.

Ask: What is your character good at? How is that shown on the page? In a romance, you can go further and ask: **What skills does your hero possess that he uses to save the heroine?**

4. **Security:** When I'm plotting, I use the element of **Security** to locate that point of no return, when a character chooses between returning to his security blanket, or changes and pushes ahead. But when I'm working on layers, I use a character's *IN-security* to discover what his worst nightmare is. What are his deepest fears? What is he going to avoid at all cost?

As I touched in developing the Noble Cause, you can discover these fears by going back to that Dark Moment in the past. At some point in your story, your hero will be pushed to his limits. In that moment, he or she will either turn back to safety, or face their fears and move forward. Discovering what he is most afraid of, what makes him feel most insecure, will add another layer to your character that will be revealed shortly before or after the dark moment.

In Donald Maass' workshops, he talks about finding that one behavior that your hero would never do. For example, building on *The Bourne Identity*, I doubt that Jason Bourne lets himself fall in love . . . and yet, there he is, falling in love with the heroine half-way through the movie.

What prompts a hero to do something he would never do?

Answer: His greatest fears pushing against him, his biggest dreams dangling before his eyes . . . and the realization that he wants something different, something more. Bringing your character to this place, and revealing this for your reader, or heroine, is a pivotal emotional point on the journey.

Ask: What is the one thing your character would never do? What would make him do it?

5. **Belonging:** In every book, there is something that keeps your character from wholeness. In an inspirational book, we often refer to this as the Lie they believe. Because of your character's darkest moment, they will have learned from it something that holds them back from happiness. We all operate with lies in our lives and your character is on this journey to be set free. So, he must learn a Truth, sometimes referred to as the Epiphany, in order to be set free to complete his mission, or to be able to love. Understanding this Lie will help you create the last layer, the one closest to his heart.

Ask: What Lie has the hero believed that has broken him?

Now, you should have interviewed your character enough to understand his Backstory, how he sees himself and why, what his motivations and goals are, what he has to live or fight for, what he's good at, what brought him to this place, what Lie he believes, and what Truth will set him free. These are the components you need to dress your character.

Your Turn:

Asking the following questions of your character will assist you in understanding him/her and gathering the pieces you need to build your romance and your layers.

For your Hero:

Basic Bio:

Name:

Age:

Profession:

Who are you? (Identity) How do you express this identity through your appearance?

What monumental event in your past shaped you and determined your goals and motivations for today? (Noble Cause/Purpose/Greatest Fear/Wound)

What are you good at? (Competence)

What is the one thing you would never do? What would make you do it? (*In*-Security)

What is the Lie that you believe? What Truth will set you free? (Belonging)

For your Heroine:

Basic Bio:

Name:

Age:

Profession:

Who are you? (Identity) How do you express this identity through your appearance?

What monumental event in your past shaped you and determined your goals and motivations for today? (Noble Cause/Purpose/Greatest Fear/Wound)

What are you good at? (Competence)

What is the one thing you would never do? What would make you do it? (*In*-Security)

What is the Lie that you believe? What Truth will set you free? (Belonging)

Why is this information important to you?

Answer: It helps you reveal the layers of your character through Essential Scenes.

Once you've built your character, it's time to insert those layer-revealing moments into your story. If you have already plotted the story, you may have already plotted these scenes. However, use these layers and essential scenes as a "checklist" to make sure you have sufficiently brought your character to life on the page.

A little author math: People often ask me about chapter and scene lengths. I have a system that works for me. I usually write a twenty chapter book. If the novel is 100,000 words in length (often the size of a historical romance), then each chapter is 5,000 words. I usually will divide the chapter in three scenes, so each scene is approximately 1500-1800 words (a solid length for a scene). Likewise, if the book is 80,000-90,000 words, (often the size of a trade romance or suspense), then I divide the book into 4,000 word chapters, with three scenes of 1200 word lengths. (Also a good size for a suspense or romance scene). This also gives me room to increase word count if I need to, based on the needs of the scene.

If the book is a category size romance, between 45,000-60,000 words, then I write approximately 3,000 word chapters and have only two scenes between 1000-1500 words.

I do this so that the percentages of the time spent in Acts 1 through 3 stay about the same. Act 1 is generally Chapters 1-3, Act 3 is generally chapters 17-20, which means that Act 2 is the remainder, usually chapters 4-16. This keeps the time spent in each act in the correct rhythm.

In order to accurately reveal character, it's helpful to use what I call, Essential Scenes.

Layer One: His Attire: (which reveals his Identity) mannerisms, clothing, public goals (Hint: Commonly this is Chapters 1-2)

In **Meet the Hero or Heroine,** you have a scene that shows:
Their Storyworld
Their Identity (that essential element that makes them who they are)
Their Goals (what they want)
The Glimpse of the Greatest Dream – We want to see what he's after, what matters to him. You do this by having him see what he wants—just a glimpse of it.
Their Competence (if you need to save word count)

Layer Two: His Behavior (which reveals Character/Values/Competence): Remember, this layer reveals how he treats people, his habits (which also reveal values), his reactions to stress (which reveal past hurts and his essential character).

- ✓ **I am good, so very good** (the scene that reveals their values and their habits)
- ✓ **Just give me my blankie** (his reactions to stress)

Layer Three: His Choices (which reveal Purpose/Noble Cause): This layer reveals his external struggles regarding plot, his greatest dreams, and why he thinks he'll never find them, and finally his obstacles to love.

There are a few scenes that accomplish this layer:

1. **If I could only** – what stands in his way to storming the castle and rescuing the princess. (Money, skills, opportunity).
2. **All I want is to be Happy** – the story about his fondest memory and why, and what his greatest dream is.
3. This may lead to **The One that Got away story** – the revelation of his past romances

Layer Four: His *In*-security: His internal struggles, greatest dreams and fears, how he feels about love, his spiritual vacancies. (This might occur anywhere from chapters 12-18.)

1. **Out of Character scene** – have the hero do something that goes contrary to his goals . . .

. . . which then leads to the

2. **What if I lose everything scene**: Have a hint of his greatest fears happen, a sort of foreshadowing of the Black Moment, and have him consider giving up.

The *Sacrificial Act* makes him heroic, but also changes him into the person he needs to be.

Layer Five: His Spiritual Lie and the discovery of the Truth.
(Often this occurs near the climatic ending, anywhere from chapters 16-20.)

1. **Breakup Scene** (when the wound is reopened)…which can be combined with the…
2. **Black Moment Event scene** (when the Greatest Fear and Lie comes true) which leads to the…
3. **Epiphany Scene** (When the Truth sets the hero/heroine free and this causes the hero/heroine to change.)

Note: Although I am writing this from the hero's perspective, these scenes apply to your heroine also.

Once you know your character's Backstory, how do you insert it?

Inserting Backstory

Shouldn't the reader know more than the characters?

Yes. *Which is the Second Key to Deeper Characterization:* **Backstory Breadcrumbs**

Creating Backstory Breadcrumbs

As you build your character and reveal his layers, you also need to keep in mind the balance between layering and dropping backstory elements that are essential to building the motivation of the character. Your reader needs to know why your character is doing something. Not an entire diary entry, but just one sentence of information—and even that should only be the barest crumb of information.

The key to Backstory is dropping just enough crumbs to stir your reader's hunger for more. You don't want to give them too much at the beginning, or they'll get filled up, satisfied, and they won't have an appetite to finish the journey.

So, how much Backstory should you put into a scene? *Just enough to give the reader the information he or she needs to understand and accept the current action and decisions.*

They just need to embrace the character's motivations for continuing on in the journey.

For example, let's say I have a character who has just inherited a ranch. I might open the scene where she is driving up to the abandoned ranch, looking at the life her uncle left her. Now, I might be tempted to go into a lengthy Backstory about how, when she was a child, she loved visiting the ranch, how she chased the prairie dogs and rode horses through the tall grasses, and how it gave her an escape from an alcoholic mother. I might go on to recall a conversation she had with her uncle, how she was like a daughter to him, and how he had one no-account son. I could even say that she'd spent the last five years as a lawyer in Minneapolis, and was burned out after winning a child abuse case, and wanted a fresh start because the case reminded her too much of her own life. I could say all that. But it's *way* too much information for the beginning of a book, and really, it gives away the punch line. We want our readers to discover all this along the way.

Instead, I'll pare it down to the essentials:

"She couldn't believe that Uncle Henry had left her the ranch instead of Billy Bob. Nor could she believe she'd abandoned her law practice, especially now, after the victories of her last case. But maybe her uncle knew her better than she knew herself, had heard the silent pleadings of her heart. Even now, the wide expanse of the blue sky filled her soul like a spring breeze after a grueling winter, drawing her back to the land."

Okay, even that might be too much, but doesn't it raise a lot more questions for the reader? What silent pleadings? What case, and why would she leave? Who is Billy Bob? And what happened as a child to keep her tethered to the land? All these questions are breadcrumbs to draw the reader further into the story.

In my book *Flee the Night*, the book opens with my heroine, Lacey on a train, sitting next to her daughter.
She sees a man get on—one Lacey recognizes as an assassin. I drop only breadcrumbs by pulling back on the information I give.

> The past couldn't have picked a worse time to find her.
>
> Trapped in seat 15A on an Amtrak Texas Eagle chugging through the Ozarks at 4:00 a.m. on a Sunday morning, Lacey . . . Galloway . . . Montgomery—what was her current last name?—tightened her leg lock around the computer bag at her feet.
>
> She dug her fingers through the cotton knit of her daughter's sweater as she watched the newest passenger to their compartment find his seat. Lanky, with olive skin and dark eyes framed in wire-rimmed glasses, it had to be Syrian assassin Ishmael Shavik, who sat down, fidgeted with his leather jacket, then impaled her with a dark glance.

In this opening scene, my heroine knows the man is after her, *but doesn't tell us why*. We also know she's protecting a briefcase, *but we don't know why*. And, we know that her past is bad, but again, *we don't know why*. All these problems are hinted at, but not solved. My goal is to lure the reader in with just enough breadcrumbs to make them hungry.

Remember: Backstory Breadcrumbs are soft, tasty, *small* morsels to lure your reader into the story.

Ask:

- ✓ What is the *essential* information the reader needs to know to give sufficient motivation for the character?

- ✓ What story questions can you drop into the scene that will keep the reader interested?

Ingredient 6: Sizzle (Dialogue!)

I'm a camping girl. I love to go out to the shore and build a blazing fire and cozy up to it. Reading good dialogue is like that campfire. It's mesmerizing, it's hot, it's attractive, and it provides light in the darkness. More than that, great dialogue is what adds the glow of romance to the story.

What is Dialogue?

Dialogue in a romance isn't just words. It's also what is *not* being said, it's body language, and internal monologue and, most of all, it's *conflict. Especially* in a romance. More than anything, dialogue moves a scene, creates emotion, reveals motivations, and produces change in a character. But good dialogue is difficult to write. Here's a hint: It's not conversation!

Okay, I admit it: Dialogue is my favorite part of a book. I just love to hear people get into arguments, dodge questions, tell it like it is, and most of all, give each other what for. Sometimes—and this is the schizophrenic writer side of me—I will even talk out loud as I'm writing dialogue, just to get the inflections. (Besides, I can say anything to myself and not get into trouble!)

But what is the secret to powerful dialogue? What's the difference between writing conversations that zing and mind-numbing dialogue that causes a book to end face down on the bureau collecting dust?

I think it's all about adding a little **Sizzle—**the element that contains attitude and energy and courage and everything your character has inside of him.

Good dialogue has four functions:

1. **Warm the Reader** (Reveal characters)

Dialogue reveals character, but only as much as the character wants to be revealed. It tells the kind of personality they are, how they feel about the people they're conversing with, where they're from, their education, their profession. Your reader should know who is speaking without any dialogue tags. Dialogue tags are used to enhance the emotions of the scene.

Keep in mind the motivations of your characters. Nobody lays it all on the line, and they'll be protecting their goals and their values and even their motivations in what they say and how they respond. Often characters don't answer the question, they pose another, or answer something else. But hidden inside their words is some sort of truth.

2. **Build the fire** (Move the plot forward)

Dialogue moves the story along by revealing information and raising new questions. If you want a fast scene, insert a lot of dialogue. If you want a slower scene, have fewer people to talk to. If you want a revealing scene, have them say something out of the ordinary—even explosive—and see what happens. It's the nugget of truth that is the purpose for the dialogue.

Which means more **Conflict**.

3. **Create Coals (**Build the foundation of the story**)**

Until you reach the happily ever after (HEA), all dialogue should deepen the conflict, create inner dissonance in the characters, and distance them from plot goals. Even if it is a sweet, romantic scene, dialogue will make them long to be together, when we know they can't be. If the hero and heroine are perfect for each other, but the hero knows there's a reason they can't be together, then that will create inner dissonance.

4. **To Illuminate** (Inform and prepare for an Epiphany)

Dialogue is a great device to lead the character into a deeper understanding of himself, and eventually lead to his Epiphany moment. Tidbits of truth, dropped and revealed along the way, will be gathered together like breadcrumbs to help him understand himself, and lead him to the *A ha!* moment!

Let's take a closer look at how to craft dialogue:

Conversation versus Dialogue, what's the difference? Conversation is what you and I have every day. Here are some recent snippets from our house:

> Mom: Hi, honey, how was school?
> Daughter: Boring.
> Mom: Did anything exciting happen today?
> Daughter: No. What's for supper?
> Mom: Hot dogs.

Daughter: Seriously?
Mom: Seriously.
Daughter: I have homework.

Okay, not riveting stuff. Except if you're in *Grey's Anatomy*.
How about my husband's recent conversation with his friend?

DH: Are you recording the game?
Friend: Yeah. But it starts at eight o'clock. Don't forget the chips.
DH: I think I'll come straight from work. Who else did you invite?
Friend: Dan. Is that okay?
DH: Maybe he can bring chips too.

Most conversation happens about unimportant, everyday things. And it's boring. Good dialogue only *seems* like real speech. Dialogue is conversation with all the boring stuff deleted—leaving only the essential, the emotional, the most dramatic words.

The last thing you want to do is to write boring dialogue. You want it to add fire for the reader, make her turn pages, make her want another confrontation. How do you make your dialogue *not* boring? Add tension! It's the heart of successful dialogue. Conflict doesn't have to be overt. Conflict can even occur in polite conversation but be in the activity behind the dialogue. I'm going to show you how to do this in just a moment.

Most early writers put conversation into their first drafts. Why? Because they want the reader to get to know the characters, they want to set the scene, and they think it's too early for conflict. *Wrong.* Every scene, every dialogue can include conflict or, like I mentioned earlier, **Sizzle**.

It makes for a handy acronym, too.

Every conversation should have:
S -- ubtexting
I – nternal monologue (includes tone of voice) -- *Attitude*
Z – ingers – words that get right to the point.
Z - eal – or the passion of each character
L – –anguage, as in body language – *Mannerisms*
E – xternal activity that matters

All these components work together, but I'm going to start with *Zeal*, or the purpose for being in the scene. Some may refer to it as the character's goals.

Zeal: Three kinds of character goals

a. **Plot goals** – Every scene is going to have plot goals. And of course, you'll have broken down your novel into chapters, each with a goal, and from there, scenes, also with a goal. And in each scene the players in the scenes will also have goals, and these goals will come across in the scene. Before you write any dialogue.

Ask: What must my character accomplish in this chapter?

b. **Emotional goals** – Your character will also have emotional goals, motivations, and desires to protect himself, or not. You know, in order to woo your reader, you'll be slowly peeling back the layers of your character to reveal his emotions. Since you don't want to reveal too much, you need to know only what he can give away for this scene.

Ask: What feelings is he going to show? What doesn't my character want others to know about him?

2. **Spiritual goals** – Finally, and especially for an inspirational book, we have spiritual goals. Even non-inspirational books have that internal "spiritual" thread, beyond emotions to the deeper questions your character will ask and the answers he/she will find. Maybe your characters don't even know what they are, but you as the author do, and a conversation will reveal those spiritual vacancies. This is part of the Illumination purpose of dialogue. Isn't it true that things come back later to haunt us? Or others drop some tidbit of truth that we remember later. You will use this when crafting your character's change and Epiphany.

Ask: What phrases or words could your hero or heroine use that you could pull in later as a memory tool?

I am going to use one of my romantic suspense books as an example. This is one of my favorite scenes from *Escape to Morning.* In this story, Search and Rescue (SAR) K-9 handler Dani Lundeen is searching for a missing girl. Undercover Homeland Security agent Will Masterson is also searching for her—but for different reasons. She is carrying important information vital to national security. He's been posing as a newspaper reporter, until he decides to strike out on his own and runs into Dani. Because he also believes there are terrorists after him and his quarry, he's garbed and armed when Dani finds him.

Plot goals: In this scene, Will is trying to find his quarry—and fast, because he believes time is running out. Dani is also trying to find the girl, but not as aggressively, because she isn't as sure the girl is lost. When Will sees Dani, he is torn. He wants to protect her, but he also wants to keep his cover and accomplish his goals.

Emotional goals: Will wants to protect Dani because he likes her. He also is afraid that once she finds out that he's been lying to her, that she'll reject him, so he wants to avoid Dani discovering the truth about him for as long as possible.

Spiritual goals: Will is aware that he isn't yet the man he hopes to be. He's trying, and he knows that God has to be in the picture for that to happen, so he needs his help.

Note: These are Will's goals, but Dani also has goals. Even though we're in Will's POV, her goals will show through. She's baffled by his attire and she suspects there is more to his story. Also, she is independent and doesn't want Will—who she believes to be a reporter—interfering with her search.

As I write this, I'm going to focus first on the words. A lot of time, because I see the activity, I write the action at the same time, but then I go through and read just the words to make sure they speak for themselves.

Here's the scene, and for study purposes, I've just used the spoken words. (By the way, if you really want to get deep with dialogue, try reading a play. The dialogue is all they have, and they have to convey every emotion through how they deliver that dialogue, and the action they put with it. Especially since it's hard to see someone's face on stage. It's a great exercise.)

Note: My explanations are in standard typestyle.

"Dani, it's okay—" (Will has just snuck up to her in the woods and is trying to keep her from being afraid, to save their relationship.)

"What part of you scaring my skin off is okay? And why do you have to always dress like a mercenary when you're in the woods? Good grief, Will, who do you think you're going to get in a fight with, a great horned owl?" (She's scared, but hiding it, and she's confused by his attire.)

"I checked this cabin. She's not here. And neither should you be." (Will, trying to get her out of the way, and moving toward safety, hopefully so he can keep on searching.)

"And, why is that, Rambo? Is that an *assault* rifle?" (Dani, angry and trying to get information out of him.)

"I'm just being prepared." (Will, trying to keep their friendship intact, trying to tell Dani about himself without giving his identity away.)

"To what, shoot and skin your own deer? With a . . . what's that, an M-16?" (She's pointing out the absurdity of the situation, and really digging for info.)

"AM4A1 carbine, sort of a mountain warfare rifle." (He's just about to reveal his identity--he so wants to be honest with her.)

"Oh, right. My mistake. I have one of those in my car, because, you know, every good woodsman *should have one.* I think you've taken this search and rescue thing too far. This is not a top-secret special ops mission. What part of this says bad guys?" (She doesn't want him interfering with her mission, and is now mad at his lies.)

"Dani, please, trust me. You need to go home and let me find this girl." (His emotional goals—for her to trust him, despite all evidence to the contrary.)

"See these little white crosses? They mean we belong out here. Our job is to *Search* and Rescue. Do you, by any chance, see a difference between, say, my outfit . . . and yours?" (Dani, now independent and back into SAR mode.)

"Okay, just yell at me when we get off the porch and back into the woods." (Will, trying to keep her safe, and get them back on course.)

"What's going on, Will?" (Dani, nearly at ultimatum point.)

"I dunno. But I do think that this girl is somewhere in one of these houses, and I can find her by myself." (Will, being as honest as he can—in hopes of accomplishing all his goals, also a hint at the spiritual lies he's been telling himself.)

"You know, I truly believe that, somehow, deep in my heart. But just for kicks, why don't we use the K-9 that we've spent a year training?" (Dani, again relying on her SAR skills.)

"Dani, please, for the last time, you need to leave." (Will, putting his primary goal on top.)

"Give me one good reason. One." (A final challenge for the truth.)

"Promise to listen to me? And, to obey me if I tell you to do something?" (Will, his emotional needs leaking out.)

"I know the words, 'you're not the boss of me,' sound slightly kindergartenish . . .but, *you're not the boss of me.* C'mon Kirby." (She's finally mad and is not going to listen.)

"You're not going anywhere without me, Dani," And I *am* the boss of you, starting right now." (Will, realizing he can't accomplish his emotional goals, and sacrificing them for the plot goal.)

I love this scene because it's a pretty unveiled scene, as far as emotions go, and I don't pull the punches with Dani. I let all her anger show through. I hope you can hear Will pleading, and then his tight voice as he finally resigns himself to the inevitable. That's a great way to add conflict to a scene: Don't pull your punches. Let your characters say what they really mean. Letting your character off his leash will cause him to say all sorts of crazy things, and create sparks that build to an inferno. And that, of course is the *Zingers* in the Sizzle. I call them Fighting Words.

What are Zingers?

Interruptions: "Dani, it's –okay—" "What part of you scaring my skin off is okay?"
Name-calling:"And, why is that, Rambo?"
Sarcasm: "I have one of those in my car, because, you know, every good woodsman *should have one.*"
Accusations: "Good grief, Will, who do you think you're going to get in a fight with, a great horned owl?"

Zingers or Fighting Words are anything that makes the dialogue sound real (only not real, as we've pointed out earlier). Think of them as the things your mother told you not to say in an argument. Here's your opportunity to say them!
However:

Avoid long narrations about information the readers already know.
Avoid giving a history lesson. Let us infer it from the dialogue

Here's a helpful technique: Find the "hook" or the zinger in every sentence, and have the characters react to that. It's sort of like a snowball picking up pieces of snow as it hurtles down the mountain.

Examples:
"I don't feel like going to school today," Sarah said, the covers pulled up to her chin. I noticed, however, that her mascara didn't bear at all the resemblance of an overnight smudge.

"School? Where *do* you feel like going today, huh? Maybe the mall?"

Or:

"I don't feel like going to school today," Sarah said, pulling the covers over her head.

"Yeah, well I don't feel like going to work, either, but that's life. Deal with it."

I used two different hooks in each sentence, and it gave each a different direction for the dialogue to go next.

But what if we don't have a big fight scene? How can we make that resonate?

I repeat: You can create tension in any scene. You just have to dig for it. Let's take a normal conversation, wrap it up in opposing goals, and see what happens.

Let's say a husband comes in from work and sees his wife dolled up and looking pretty. He's too tired to go out, but they had a fight this morning, so he wants to make nice. But he also is hiding the fact that at work he was really tempted to go out with his beautiful new female partner because his wife has been so distant lately, and he is feeling guilty about that.

So, underneath the surface, he wants a reason to 1. Get mad and justify his temptation, or 2. Just get through the night without a fight.

Meanwhile, his wife, who has been home with the kids all day, is feeling ugly and desperately wants to make up with her hubby. And she suspects that he might be seeing someone else, and just wants to see that he cares.

So, their dialogue might play out like this:

Foundational Conversation:

"What's the occasion?" he asks. (I'm not sure what to expect.)
"No occasion. Just wanted to look nice. How was work?" (Don't I look nice? Don't you notice me?)

"You always look nice." (Don't ask me about work, I don't want to be reminded of what I nearly did. Another great dialogue device: dodging the question.)

"The baby spit up on my other outfit." (I was home, all day, taking care of the kids. I need some encouragement.)

"What's for supper?" (He's hinting that he doesn't want to go out.)

"I haven't even thought about it, what with Jimmy's soccer club and Amy's school project. And I have choir practice tonight." (Family, church, responsibilities—see, someone has to take care of them!) "I s'pose I could throw in a frozen pizza, again."

"We had that last night." (Nothing will ever change.)

"So, you don't want pizza?" (You don't want me, even though I work so hard to take care of you and the kids?)

"It's not really about what I want, is it? But what we have. Pizza is fine." (I'm stuck in this relationship. In this life).

"By the way, I don't want pizza either. But the kids do, and that's what matters." (I'm not happy in this relationship, either, but for the kids, we'll stay together).

Now, that seems like boring dialogue, but set against their goals and motivations, there is a lot being said. It's just that it is all underneath the surface. It doesn't matter what POV we are in, we understand exactly what they are saying if we look beneath the surface. However, this dialogue needs work, so we're going to ramp it up with external conflict, just on that first layer. We'll do this by adding in some Fighting Words, some *Zingers.*

Zinger-added dialogue:

"You look real nice. What's the occasion?" he asks.

"No occasion. Just wanted to look nice. How was wor--?" (***First Zinger – interruption)***

"You always look nice."

"The baby spit up on my other outfit."

"What's for supper?"

"I haven't even thought about it, what with Jimmy's soccer club and Amy's school project. And I have choir practice tonight. I s'pose I could throw in a frozen pizza, again."

"We had that last night."

(Now, here come the accusation Zingers)

"And your point? You don't want pizza? Maybe you don't want a pretty wife, either, or clean kids. Maybe you want to go back to work!"

"It's not really about what I want, is it? But what we have. Pizza is fine. Just perfect."

"For your information, I don't want pizza either. But the kids do, and that's what matters."

Note, this is the same foundational dialogue, except I added just a few more confrontational words. And suddenly, the tension increased. We could go the other way with it too, and add a different kind of tension.

Alternate Zinger Dialogue:

"What's the occasion?" he asks.

"No occasion. Just wanted to look nice. How was work?"

"You always look nice."

"I do? The baby spit up on my other outfit."

(See how that little, "I do?" interjects vulnerability? That's a Zinger of a different sort. It jolts the conversation out of the ordinary.)

"Of course. Even with spit-up. What's for supper?"

(And of course, what he says softens the conversation even more.)

"I haven't even thought about it, what with Jimmy's soccer club and Amy's school project. And I have choir practice tonight. I s'pose I could throw in a frozen pizza, again."

"We had that last night."

"So, you don't want pizza? I don't know–"

"Pizza is more than fine, honey. Just perfect, really."

"By the way, I don't want pizza either. But the kids do, and that's what matters. I'll throw some extra pepperoni on, just for you."

Same motivations, but different outcomes, with a few tweaks. The thing is, behind every line there is a motivation, a meaning, and you need to keep the goals of the conversation for each character in front of you as you write.

But even this is just mundane dialogue until I add another two elements of Sizzle: **External Activity and Body Language**

Every dialogue scene has to have *activity that contains meaning.* When we are in a scene, just to have them reacting with their body or tone makes for a mundane scene. A person can only smile so much. So you want to wrap up their words in actions that deepen their words. Give them something to do that accentuates their words: kneading bread, as she's keeping her voice light and telling her husband that it's just fine that he came home hours late without calling is a great way to convey that no, it's not all well, as she pounds the bread to a pulp. Then, when you add body language, it means something.

Here are three lines from a snippet of dialogue without the External Actions and Body Language

"I don't care where you're going. Stay out all night if you want to. In fact, I hope you have a great time."

Simple dialogue, but now let's add actions that contain meaning and some frugal body language:

"I don't care where you're going." Janice barely looked up from her book as he stood by the door. "Stay out all night if you want to." She put a thumb over the paragraph to keep her place. Looked up and smiled—the kind of smile she used to give him when she did trust him. When he deserved her trust. "In fact, I hope you have a great time."

He closed the door, hating himself as it latched behind him.

Notice that she doesn't even use tone of voice, just her actions show that she's reached a point of not caring. Now, let's look at another way, same words:

"I don't care where you're going." Janice dumped the baked potatoes into the garbage. "Stay out all night if you want to." She flashed him a smile as she threw the casserole pan into the sink, turned on the water full blast. She forced herself not to wince as it splashed her face. "In fact, I hope you have a great time." She grabbed the towel and very, very slowly, wiped her face, keeping the towel there until she heard the soft click of the door closing behind her husband.

Okay, one of the differences is that these are in two different POVs. Again, I didn't use any voice tones, just actions behind the words and the barest amount of body language.

Note: The right balance between meaningful action and body language will *feel* natural. Try to balance them out with two to three sentences of meaningful action, with body language thrown in now and again to see their face. Most of the time, however, you want the action to speak just as loudly as the words.

Let's take our earlier scene and add meaningful action and body language;

Frank came in, plopping his briefcase on the counter. "What's the occasion?" He pulled off his tie, picked up the mail, sorted through it.

Janice smoothed her dress, took a breath. "No occasion. I just wanted to look nice. How was wor--?"

"You always look nice." He held up an envelope to the light, squinting.

Janice picked up an onion, started to chop it for the casserole she was making for church. "The baby spit up on my other outfit."

"What's for supper?"

She wiped her eyes as they began to water.

"I haven't even thought about it, what with Jimmy's soccer club and Amy's school project. And I have choir practice tonight. I s'pose I could throw in a frozen pizza again." She didn't turn toward him, just sniffed as she scraped the onions into a bowl, then chucked the knife and the cutting board into the sink.

"We had that last night." He set the mail down, thumbed open yet another offering of a low-rate credit card. Shook his head.

"So you don't want pizza?" She turned, reached for a towel, and when she couldn't find one, wiped her hands on the hem of her dress.

"It's not really about what I want, is it? But what we have." He looked up, for the first time finding her eyes.

She shrugged, picking up thc bowl of onions, staring into it.

"Pizza is fine." He picked up his briefcase, tucking the mail into his jacket pocket.

"By the way, I don't want pizza either." She opened the freezer and wiggled out the crushed boxes from the crammed freezer. "But the kids do, and that's what matters."

We sense his indifference to her, the feeling that he's more interested in junk mail than her. And she is trying to hide her feelings, masking it with chopping the onions. Her pulling the boxes out of a freezer already full of frozen dinners tells us that they don't eat out as often as she hopes.

Now we're going to add another element of Sizzle: *Internal Monologue and Tone of Voice.* This is all about attitude.

Good internal thought should be interspersed lightly, but be only the thoughts the POV character would think. Same goes with tone of voice: sparingly, but with impact. Your tone of voice is actually an extension of the thoughts, so often it's not even necessary. Also, one of the fun parts of interspersing internal monologue is that your character can be saying one thing and thinking something totally different. His tone of voice can convey that.

A few pointers about Internal Monologue.

First of all, you're in a character's POV, so anything they think, if it doesn't have quotation marks around it, is internal and ***should not be in italics***. The only time you need italics is when the character is remembering another voice in their head, or they are unable to voice the words they are speaking. For example if a person is remembering something their mother said to them. Or if they are watching someone leave from across the room and are unable to say, *Stop, don't go!* although they are screaming it in their head.

> ***Think of internal monologue as screaming, or another voice speaking inside your head, and you'll get it right.***

Now that the italic issue is settled, here are my rules of thumb when using internal monologue:

Example: *I really don't want her to leave, because if she does leave I'll be alone and back where I started.*

This thought feels jarring for the reader, and frankly, carries less of an impact.

Try: He didn't want her to leave. Not really. Because then where would he be?

Do you see the difference? This allows the reader to sympathize with him, in fact, the reader knows him better than he knows himself at this point, which is fun for the reader.

Same goes for things like *he thought* or *he wondered.* You know who is thinking the thought, so it's not necessary.

Example: Did he really want her to leave? No, he thought.

Try: Did he really want her to leave? No.

What about internal introspection? I sometimes use italics during an Epiphany, when a character is **remembering something he or she said, or something someone said to them**. This qualifies as another voice in their head. But even then, I put the dialogue piece of memory in italics, and keep the introspection in regular thoughts. In other words, if you're writing in third person, just write the character's thoughts in third person.

Not: He always took a good thing and tore it to pieces, he thought about himself.

Better: He always took a good thing and tore it to pieces.

You can give it even more impact by converting interior monologue into a question.

Not: He wondered why he always took a good thing and tore it to pieces.

Better: Why did he always take a good thing and tear it to pieces?

Let's take a look at how internal monologue works in our Janice and Frank "Marriage Blues" scene:

Frank came in, plopping his briefcase on the counter. “What’s the occasion?” He pulled off his tie, picked up the mail, sorted through it.

Of course there had to be an occasion. Because she couldn’t dress up for any other reason, could she? Janice smoothed her dress, took a breath. “No occasion. I just wanted to look nice. How was wor--?”

“You always look nice.” He held up an envelope to the light, squinting.

Yeah, sure she looked nice. Couldn’t he just speak the truth? What had happened that their entire marriage had reduced to lies? Janice picked up an onion, started to chop it for the casserole she was making for church. “The baby spit up on my other outfit.” Her eyes began to burn. Those onions.

“What’s for supper?”

No, oh, “I’m sorry honey, is the baby sick?” Or “how was your day?” Just supper, and maybe later, “Where are my clean sweatpants?” She wiped her eyes as they began to water.

“I haven’t even thought about it, what with Jimmy’s soccer club and Amy’s school project. And I have choir practice tonight. I s’pose I could throw in a frozen pizza again.” She didn’t turn toward him, just sniffed as she scraped the onions into a bowl, then chucked the knife and the cutting board into the sink.

“We had that last night.” He set the mail down, thumbed open yet another offering of a low-rate credit card. Shook his head.

“So, you don’t want pizza?” She couldn’t help the shrill in her voice—well, she could. But he deserved it. She turned, reached for a towel, and when she couldn’t find one, wiped her hands on the hem of her dress.

“It’s not really about what I want, is it? But what we have.” He looked up, for the first time finding her eyes.

She stared at him, his words echoing inside her. What *did* they have? She shrugged, picking up the bowl of onions, staring into it.

“Pizza is fine.” He picked up his briefcase, tucking the mail into his jacket pocket.

Perfect, just perfect. “By the way, I don’t want pizza either.” She whispered, her voice on the fine edge of breaking. She opened the freezer and wiggled out the crushed boxes from the crammed freezer. “But the kids do, and that’s what matters.”

See how the internal monologue and frugal, yet strong use of tone of voice deepen the scene?

That's a scene with all the elements of *Sizzle*. What you didn't realize is that I took mundane conversation, and because of the motivations, the conflict underneath, the action with meaning, the body language, the internal monologue, I also turned it into a passage of **subtexting**. Their entire marriage is about disappointment, and how they've grown apart, and this scene about what to have for dinner represents exactly that problem.

What is subtexting?

Subtexting is layering in meaning, using the dialogue or setting as metaphor for the deeper meaning of the scene.

Subtexting can be accomplished without dialogue through the use of setting and action.

In the scene above, I subtexted with action set against the words. I used the onions to show the tears, the junk mail to accentuate what fills their lives, and the crammed box of pizza to represent how wrecked she feels.

Another way to subtext is through setting. It's the use of rich, vivid nouns and powerful verbs to set an emotional tone to the scene. In the next scene, there is little dialogue, but hopefully you can sense the mood of the POV character through the setting.

(From *Taming Rafe*, this scene is set in the Dust Bowl of Wyoming, 1930, and is right after the death of Mary's husband. Her widower-landlord has offered her the option of marriage in order to support her and her child.)

They pulled up to the unpainted house. It sat in a dip between two weather-beaten, grassless hills. The effects of the last dust storm had piled dirt against the barn and porch. Dirty curtains flapped from the open windows, and a pot of dead geraniums told her that Mrs. Thatcher—God rest her soul—had been a woman of hope.

Matthias's bulk jiggled the car as he got out. "Preacher's inside. Hurry up."

Mary thought he might grab her case from the jump seat, but he marched into the house without so much as a glance backward.

She had no time for tears. Rosie needed a home. She needed work. Mary eased open the door. Weakness rushed through her, a ripple of despair that had the ability to crumple her. She couldn't do this. A tear squeezed out, and she wiped it against Rosie's head, brushing her lips against her daughter's skin.

"Mary!" Thatcher stood on the porch, the preacher behind him.

She saw anger in his eyes and stiffened. *Please, Lord, help me.*

"Can I get your case for you, ma'am?" The voice beside her, a soft drawl, seemed calm against her racing heart.

We don't insert even a tone of voice, but the setting tells us everything we need to know about her emotions and even the tension that is building for later.

Building on what we know, let's take another look at the Will and Dani scene—with all the elements of *Sizzle* added:

"Dani, it's okay," Will said, trying to keep his voice low, scanning his gaze past her, toward the cabin, past it into the dark fold of forest. (Setting subtexting used to accentuate the danger. What is lurking there?)

"What part of you scaring my skin off is okay?" Her voice shrilled, matching the white panic that hued her face. "And why do you have to always dress like a mercenary when you're in the woods? Good grief, Will, who do you think you're going to get in a fight with, a great horned owl?"

He couldn't hide the smile, nor it seemed his emotions. He'd seen her sneak up, and totally turned off the common sense screaming in his brain.

No, he hadn't expected to fight with anyone—least of all the woman he couldn't seem to ditch.

"I checked this cabin. She's not here. And neither should you be."

Her face told him exactly how utterly odd his words sounded. "And, why is that, Rambo?" Her eyes widened and she reached for the house, as if to brace herself. "Is that an *assault* rifle?"

He slung it off his shoulder, set it away from him, from her. Why, oh why couldn't he let her simply knock on the door, find nothing, and leave? He could have stayed hidden.

And then he'd have two women to protect . . . Dannette and Amina, if he ever found her. "I'm just being prepared."

"To what, shoot and skin your own deer? With a . . . what's that, an M-16?"

"AM4A1 carbine, sort of a mountain warfare rifle."

"Oh, right, my mistake. I have one of those in my car, because, you know, every good woodsman *should have one*." She had real fire in those eyes and she didn't look in the least amused by her own joke. "I think you've taken this search and rescue thing too far. This is not a top-secret special ops mission." She turned and held her hand out to the scenery. Shadows pressed through the trees, striping the yard like a prison fence. "What part of this says bad guys?"

Whoa, she was cute when she was sarcastic. But at the moment he couldn't give into the desire to laugh because she was so utterly wrong it hurt him right in the middle of his chest.

"Dani, please, trust me. You need to go home and let me find this girl."

She frowned at him. Pointed to her orange jacket, then the shabrack vest on her new dog—now where had she conjured up a new K-9 so quickly? "See these little white crosses? They mean we belong out here. Our job is to *Search* and Rescue. Do you, by any chance, see a difference between, say, my outfit . . . and yours?"

He smirked, but picked up his weapon and took her by the arm. "Okay, just yell at me when we get off the porch and back into the woods."

This night had started out dark, and was only worsening as he moved into daylight. He'd driven up to the rest area and to his dismay, saw that the T's vehicle still hadn't moved.

Not good. Not good.

Hoping to cut off the distance between the T's and the cabin, he'd tracked back and used another forest service road to wind into the Tom Lake area.

"What's going on, Will?" Dani said as she yanked her arm out of his grip. "Don't tell me you were the scent Kirby found?"

He made a face. "I dunno. But I do think that this girl is somewhere in one of these houses, and I can find her by myself."

She gave a harsh laugh. "You know, I truly believe that, somehow, deep in my heart. But just for kicks, why don't we use the K-9 that we've spent a year training?"

He shook his head, turned and headed for the tree cover, a bittersweet hope that she'd follow. Because, he didn't really want to throw her over his shoulder and haul her out of danger, like a *real* boy scout.

Okay, maybe a little.

But the fact that Little Miss SAR was back, an obviously fully charged, meant trouble.

And even more dangerous were the little feelings of happiness that were exploding all over his heart.

Bad Will. Bad, Bad Will.

Still as she followed him into the forest, stood there with her hands on her hips, her eyebrows up, he just wanted to reach over and hug her.

"Dani, please, for the last time, you need to leave."

"Give me one good reason." She held up one elegant finger. "One."

Okay, she had a point . . . without knowing it. He couldn't rightly explain without blowing his cover. But without blowing his cover, he couldn't get her to leave.

Besides, what if she were caught hiking out?

Maybe it would be better if he just . . . hung around, or vice versa.

"Promise to listen to me? And, to obey me if I tell you to do something?"

She looked at him like he'd turned purple and spoken Russian.

"I know the words, 'you're not the boss of me,' sound slightly kindergartenish . . . but, *you're not the boss of me.*" She turned to her new K-9, sitting beside her and eyeing him like a moldy sirloin. "C'mon, Kirby."

This time he really did stop her. Put all one-hundred-ninety pounds between her and her exit, and wore a face he hadn't used for quite some time. Maybe three years. "You're not going anywhere without me, Dani," he said, slow and dangerously. (Note: This is the only tone of voice he uses.) "And I *am* the boss of you, starting right now."

How do you build your own dialogue *Sizzle*?

When you're building dialogue, ask:

- ✓ What do the hero and heroine each need to accomplish, and what emotions will they be showing?
- ✓ What do they really want to say? (Don't go with your first instinct. Write their true emotions.)
- ✓ What could they be doing that either accentuates their words, or puts them in relief?
- ✓ What is the appropriate body language for their attitude and what could they be hiding?
- ✓ What setting could accentuate the mood or tone of the scene?
- ✓ What is the one tone of voice you could insert that would add impact?
- ✓ Is there a metaphor in this scene that betrays the theme of the scene? How can you deepen that metaphor through action, setting, props, or words?

Here's an idea: Write the dialogue, and then go through it and ramp it up, adding in the subtexting, the meaningful action, and especially the Zingers. Don't expect to get it right the first time, but keep laying, adding in more Zingers, more conflict until it comes to life. And if you have dialogue that seems to fall flat—dissect it. You may be missing the *Sizzle*!

And here's a final caveat: Keep the tone of voice spare, but with impact.

He snarled.
He muttered.
He snapped.
He growled.

But, please not:
He laughed (as a dialogue tag. Okay as a sentence)
He stammered. (You can write the stammering words instead).
He smiled. (Again, *not* a dialogue tag).
But, I'll let you use *he whispered.* Maybe. Once.

Just say: *he said* and *she said.* And fill in the rest.

Ingredient 7: It's Just a Little Kiss

Have you ever entered a writing contest? The tension starts building after you've submitted your manuscript for judging. Yes, you want to create the best entry you can, and you work hard on, even worry about, your sentences and story structure. But second thoughts and wringing hands don't set in until *after* you've submitted. Why? Because you're hoping for a great outcome and your fears about your manuscript—the frailties you recognize, or don't recognize in your writing—are shouting at you that you might not succeed. The more you continue to write, the more you fall in love with storycrafting, the more you invest into the process, and the more you see the hope of publication, the more you want it. Hence, the more the tension increases.

Put that same "want" into a romance and you have sexual tension! It's a key element of romance: that hope of a kiss, or more. You can't write a romance without at least a nod to this tension.

Sexual tension in a novel is that hope and desire for affection that builds into each kiss or physical act of affection. It's different for each genre, and of course the two different markets—American Booksellers Association (ABA) or general market or Christian Booksellers Association (CBA) or inspirational market.

In the general market, you have everything from sweet romance, which might have a sex scene, (but it would either be behind closed doors or very tame,) to erotic, where nothing is behind closed doors. You can have erotic romantic suspense or erotic historical or sweet romantic suspense and sweet historical and everything in between. It's almost a given in today's general market that regardless of genre there will be some sort of romantic thread, and that it will culminate in physical affection to some degree.

For all genres in the CBA) we close the door. We also keep the scenes fairly chaste, with affection being limited to kissing and not much beyond that.

There are writers out there that push this envelope a bit. As a writer, you have to do what is comfortable for you, and appropriate for the story. I always remind myself that my mother is reading these books. That helps me know where I feel comfortable drawing the line. But, whether you have just kissing, or you have what I call the "trigonometry" on the page, you still need to know how to reel out the tension.

And frankly, sexual tension in a CBA novel can be just as strong as a general market novel if it is done right.

How do we create sexual tension in a book, and when do we use it? I'm going to break sexual tension apart into components, and then we'll talk about how and when to weave it into the story.

The Components of Sexual Tension (We'll expand on these in a moment.)

1. **The Wishing: The Pull toward each other, or setting the kindling for the attraction.**
   The Wanting – This is about building the romance, or the physical and emotional Why's of being together.
   The Work – This is the Investment of the romance, the more the characters are willing to let each other into their lives.
   The What-if – this is what they want, and getting enough of a taste of it to build hope.

2. **The Waiting: The Push away from each other, or creating tension.**
   The Walls – This includes the External Obstacles and the Internal Obstacles (and especially the hint of the wound)

3. **The Wink: The first kiss, or a taste of the affection**
   The Warning- this is a larger hint of the wound, or even a slight reopening of the wound.

4. **The Wonderful: The full-out kiss!**

Let's examine these elements:

The Wishing

The components of great sexual tension start with the Wishing—or the desire. The more our characters wish for romance, affection, and a happily ever after, the stronger the tension will become. Think of the wish as the buildup of steam. ☺ Or perhaps water pressure against a dam. I usually put it in terms of the *Pull* toward the object of their affection. The Pull takes on three different forms:

The Wanting – The characters must enjoy spending time together. Sure, they might have obstacles to love, but even the sparks produced should be relatively enjoyable, like a good fight. As the romance progresses, the hero and heroine should have an increasing awareness that they like each other. They enjoy each other's personalities, or wisdom, or spiritual insights, or sense of humor, or strength—whatever it might be as the story unrolls. (You'll be creating those "Why" moments we touched on earlier.) They will also become more physically aware of each other—from

their initial beauty to imagining what it might be like to be in their arms, to wanting to be there! The author's job is to increase the Wanting, both emotionally and physically.
One of the best movies for romantic tension is *Dirty Dancing.* In *Dirty Dancing,* the first step of the Wanting is when Baby sees Johnny dance with his dance partner. You can almost see the longing written on Baby's face. Then, she even gets a taste of what it might be like to be with him when he asks her to dance that first night when she "carries in a watermelon." He leaves her breathless and alone on the dance floor . . . wanting more.

The Work – The characters should fall prey to the law of increasing rewards. This means the more they get to know each other, the more they invest, and even if they haven't received the "reward," they don't want to turn around for the hope of something that lies ahead. A marathon works in this fashion. The further a runner progresses toward the end, the more the power of what they've already accomplished pushes them, in tandem with the reward that is promised when they finish the marathon.

If we apply this principle to a romance, the hero and heroine will continue to discover each other's "layers,", and find the "treasures" inside each layer. As they discover the increasing value of each other, the idea of not being with each other, even if they still have considerable obstacles, will seem more and more horrible. The reward pulls them, and the investment in the relationship pushes them through the obstacles. The key to successful Work is a slow "unlayering" of the characters, as well as an appreciation of each layer.

In *Dirty Dancing* there is a lot of Work involved as they learn the dance. They slowly invest in each other with the goal of dancing. Then, when Baby finds out about Penny, she gets even more involved in Johnny's world. Baby is pulled deeper and deeper into his life and begins to know him beyond his playboy image.

The What-if – Your hero and heroine should also begin to picture what it might be like to kiss, or to be in each other's arms, or imagine a relationship with the other person. It will start with the What-if of a kiss, and lead to more as the story progresses, but giving the hero and heroine a picture of the reward helps it to have more power.

The What-if in *Dirty Dancing* is perfect. First Baby wishes to dance like Johnny and his partner, then to be in his arms, and it cumulates when Baby finally dances as his partner at the nightclub. Afterward, as they sit in the car together, Baby says "We were great. We pulled it off." She has started to see them as a team.

The **Wanting**, or the pull toward each other, is just one half of Sexual Tension. We also need the *push away* from each other or the fear of loss, if we want to create adequate pressure. Think of the push away as the wall of the dam that keep the romantic flood waters from breaking free. Or the lid on the pressure cooker, holding in the steam. The Wanting can be expressed through what I call **The Waiting.**

The Waiting is that time period where you are building to the first kiss, but you are still keeping the hero and heroine apart, in terms of their physical affection. This first element of keeping them separated can be termed **The Walls**.

The first set of **Walls** between your hero and heroine are those *External Obstacles*—or Why Nots—that we've set up between the hero and heroine. What physical elements in the plot keep these people apart? We've outlined them earlier, but just as a review, here's some that I've used:

- ✓ She's the fire chief, he's a volunteer firefighter. (*The Perfect Match*)
- ✓ She's a reporter (undercover) intent on proving he's guilty of a crime. (*Reclaiming Nick*)
- ✓ He's the cop who arrests her. (*Nothing but Trouble*)
- ✓ She's a bookstore owner, he's her new handyman who she thinks is sabotaging her. (*Happily Ever After*)

In *Dirty Dancing*, the Walls, are, of course, the fact that Baby is a guest and Johnny is a staffer—and rather low on the totem pole too. Plus, he's not one of the frat boys; he's from the wrong side of the tracks.

These obstacles are key to keeping the hero and heroine from throwing themselves into each others' arms. However, as the story progresses, these External Obstacles will feel less important than their love. This is where *Internal Obstacles* come in. Underlying the External Obstacles will be the hint of a bigger issue, usually something from the characters' past that make them afraid of love. (The wound !) Maybe they lost their first love, or maybe they caused the death of someone they loved, or maybe they come from a broken home. Whatever the Internal Obstacle is, it conspires to keep them apart on both an emotional and physical level. This wound is a much stronger Wall, and will be the hero's and heroine's last line of defense before the outer walls to their heart are breached. For now, however, smaller Internal Obstacles conspire to hold them back.

Eventually (usually about half-way through the book), they can't hold back any longer, they have what I call **The Wink**. This is that tentative, or quick, or accidental, or even purposeful-but-mistaken first kiss. It acts as a taste of hope, a taste of what could be.

Here's a secret: The timing of this kiss is essential because once you allow them the kiss, *tension deflates.* I often wait for that moment when the tension feels unbearable, that moment that it feels natural for them to kiss—and then I hold them back! I wait until the next chapter. And then I give them just a taste so I don't deflate the tension. I leave the characters (and the reader) wanting more.

In *Dirty Dancing*, you might think they skip **The Wink** and go right to the big event. The tension has been building for so long, we feel like they have already kissed. But the Wink can be something that acts like kiss—a moment of recognized attraction. So, for Baby and Johnny, you could say the dance was really the Wink. In many general market books, they also skip the kiss and go right to the main event, but even that first main event is just a taste of the real thing they'll have when they *truly* declare their love. If you read any general market romances, you'll note that after the Wink, or that first physical encounter, regardless of what it is, it always causes more stress, more angst, more longing, and even a healthy dose of regret. But it does serve to tantalize the reader to want more.

Now that we've had the taste of the happy ending, **The Wish** becomes overwhelming. The hero and heroine want to be with each other, they have worked to get to know each other, and they've gotten a taste of the What-if.

About three chapters later, it's time for **The Wow**. This is the amazing, we-waited-for-it kiss! The one with all the pent-up passion, and in general market stories, often more happens than just a kiss. But this *Wow* is there to cement in the hero's and heroine's minds that the wonderful ending they're hoping for is not far away.

In *Dirty Dancing,* we have the *Wow* in the old house when she goes to him after her father rejects him. Baby and Johnny are dancing, until . . . yes, it's a strong scene that we all remember.

But just because they've had the *Wow* doesn't mean they're going to have their happy ending yet. That's part of the romance. We give them what they want, and then make them fight for it. We're now going to employ some Push-Pull to create tension, so we'll return to some of the elements we employed in the wishing and waiting stages.

First, we want to make the hero and heroine wish for more—a real future this time. They need to wonder what Happily Ever After might look like with the other person. They need to talk to their friends about this, and even visualize it to the point where they thirst for it.

In *Dirty Dancing* we see scenes where Baby and Johnny are in bed, the rain falling around them, and she's wishing they could be together, have a happy ending. But, of course it's not to be. They still have those Internal Obstacles keeping them apart.

However, if it's that easy, then there is no tension! So, you need to hold them back with a final warning. **The Warning** is that Internal Obstacle—or wound—that suddenly becomes so overwhelming that it feels insurmountable. Often the Warning happens right before the Black Moment and cumulates in the Breakup. It's in this stage that the hero and heroine are made to believe that they can't overcome the Internal Obstacle to love.

In *Dirty Dancing* this Warning comes when Johnny is accused of stealing and he's fired, even though he's exonerated. His wound is opened : He'll always be "trash" from the wrong side of the tracks. He gives into this wound and leaves.

Of course, true love will win the day, and that's when **The Wonderful** happens. After the breakup, the hero and heroine will realize that the Whys of their relationship are stronger than the Why Nots, and this arms them to make the Big Gesture/Sacrifice to prove their love to each other. (We'll expand on that more in a moment.)

In *Dirty Dancing,* this scene is obvious. "Nobody puts Baby in a corner!" Johnny walks into the final performance of the season and dances "his way," pulling Baby on the stage with him in their triumphant moment where they are truly partners. When we dive into the next section, our plot building activities, we'll overlay romance structure on top of basic story structure and incorporate the Black Moment/Lie and the Truth that sets them free, into this triumphant Happily Ever After moment.

I've had the time of my life. And with the right kiss, all that tension was worth it.

It's not just a kiss!

How do you write a great kiss? A great kiss (or more) in a romance is about slowing the act down, letting the reader experience it, taking them back to the moments of their own great kisses. It's not just about mechanics, but the senses, and most of all, the *impact* of the kiss.

Just to review quickly: Here are the three kisses in a romance (and if you are writing a romance in the general market, you can extrapolate from there. ☺):

Kiss One: An introductory "I didn't mean to, did we just do that?" Kiss

Kiss Two: An "I really want to kiss you now and I'm going to" Kiss

Kiss Three: An "I love you, and I mean it" Kiss

Now, let's explore the "hows" of a great kiss.

1. **A kiss should be savored.**

Again, don't rush the act of the kiss. We don't need to know every sloppy detail, but the mechanics of his hands, his eyes, and how he or she eases into this kiss is important. It's like holding your breath. Draw the kiss out to build expectation.

2. **A kiss should be experienced.**

A great kiss isn't just shown, it's experienced. A great kiss uses the five senses to help the reader understand it. Use your five senses. Tell the reader how the heroine smells, or how she feels, i.e. *he ran his hand over her smooth skin.* Go ahead and comment on the fact he just drank coffee or the salt of the heroine's tears (i.e. taste). Sometimes, my heroes or heroines even make sweet noises of appreciation. And of course, they should see the kiss in each other's eyes.

3. **A kiss should make an impact.**

The point of the kiss is to cause more tension. Sure, the sexual tension is momentarily released, but the fact of the kiss raises new internal and external conflict. There will always be a response to a great kiss, something that stays with them until at least the next chapter, if not longer. Especially for the first kiss, have an immediate response—and then a later response when they are alone and ready to contemplate the meaning of the kiss.

Let's take a look at some examples.

This is Kiss #1 for my book *Point of No Return*, my January 2011 Love Inspired Suspense (LIS).

> Mae's chest burned. "Why did you come back?"
>
> His eyes caught hers, his voice so low it felt more like a breath, whispered deep inside her chest. "You can't figure that out, Mae? You can't?"

And then, as she wanted to hurt him or hold him or do anything to calm the whir of panic inside, he reached out and wrapped his hand around her neck, pulled her to himself, and kissed her.

It wasn't a gentle, tentative kiss either, like it had been that night on the balcony, or even a hello, slightly sad kiss like the one he'd given her before he broke her heart in Moscow.

No, this kiss tasted of desperation and regret, of missing her, and needing her, and as he pulled her tighter, she needed him right back. His lips were sweet orange and spicy halva, tasting of everything she'd remembered and more.

And for a second, she did nothing. Didn't move, didn't breathe. Just tried to understand exactly who this man was . . .

Then, it didn't matter. He wrapped his arms around her, she curled hers around his shoulders and she let herself kiss him with everything she wanted and everything she'd lost, deepening her kiss and forgetting how infuriating and bossy and overprotective and—

"I'm sorry." He broke away, and brought his hand to cradle her jaw, his blue eyes in hers. "I'm so sorry."

Oh no, not again . . .

Let's break it apart a bit.

First, we have some sparks: **"You can't figure that out, Mae? You can't?"**

Those are Fighting Words. Accusatory. Breathtaking.

Then, we have the action of him kissing her. I just state it. Sometimes people write, "His lips met hers," or even, "He leaned forward, touching her with his lips." Whatever you want to do. Just tell us what's going on. Don't get too poetic or we'll get confused and won't get to the good part . . . the savoring.

Then, tell us about the kiss. I use an intro phrase here: **It wasn't a gentle, tentative kiss either. No, this kiss tasted of desperation and regret, of missing her, and needing her,**

Then I throw in a sense: taste. **His lips were sweet orange and spicy halva, tasting of everything she'd remembered and more**

And finally I move into the effect of the kiss: Then, it didn't matter . . .

She let herself kiss him with everything she wanted and everything she'd lost, deepening her kiss and forgetting how infuriating and bossy and overprotective and—

Now, since this was the intro kiss, I needed it to end with an "Uh oh, what did we just do" moment…

"I'm sorry." He broke away, and brought his hand to cradle her jaw, his blue eyes in hers. "I'm so sorry."

Oh no, not again . . .

Let's look at another one. This is the middle kiss—the one where it is right and good with the world. (Before the Breakup).

Her eyes searched his, a pain, or hope in them so tender it nearly broke his heart. "I do need you, Chet. I do need you."

And of course, those words coming out of her mouth as she sat in the swaddle of his arms, the sun backlighting the sky, her beautiful green eyes in his . . . he traced his gaze around her face and stopped there, at her incredible mouth.

What was a guy to do? He caught his breath, met her eyes for a yes, then kissed her. Sweetly, touching his mouth to hers, testing, then tasting her tears. She didn't move toward him, but she lifted her face, and he curved his hand around her neck, deepening his kiss ever so slowly. Something about her surrender made him want to weep. Tough, beautiful Mae, needing him . . . Oh, *Mae*. He didn't hurry, just explored her mouth, then broke away to kiss her cheekbones, her forehead, her eyes, one then the other, then, finally, *finally,* back to her lips.

She sighed in his arms, a slow shudder that seemed a release of something she'd been holding tight, and when he broke the kiss, touching his forehead to hers, she looked at him, and smiled.

Smiled.

He traced it with his finger. "I need you too, babe."

Note again the steps:
Sparks—or a bit of conversation that arrests our attention. How often do we say we need each other? **"I do need you, Chet. I do need you."**

The movement/action of the kiss: **He caught his breath, met her eyes for a yes, then kissed her.**

I have a bit of taste: **then tasting her tears**

And then the effect of the kiss: **Tough, beautiful Mae, needing him . . . Oh, *Mae***
And . . . **She sighed in his arms, a slow shudder that seemed a release of something she'd been holding tight**

Finally, the end. Remember, this is a happy kiss:

When he broke the kiss, touching his forehead to hers, she looked at him, and smiled.

Smiled.

He traced it with his finger. "I need you too, babe."

Now, just a note about the senses. You don't have to use taste. You can also use smell, and touch and sound.

Here's another kiss example. This one is from *Mission: Out of Control*, also a LIS about a bodyguard who falls in love with his client, a rock star. Try and figure out what kiss it is…the first, second or last?

"Brody."

"Don't talk."

Wow. He pulled her down the darkened street, and now he was scaring her. "Brody, what's the matter?"

He stopped then, rounded on her as if he had something to say. But whatever it was, the words wouldn't make it past his mouth, his shaking head.

And then, just like that, he kissed her. Just put his mouth on her lips, hard and fast, and practically inhaling her as he pushed her against the stone wall of some ancient building.

Brody—?

He had the most amazing smell—the sun on his skin, his after shave, and a late afternoon stubble that made her bring her fingers to it, rub them through it.

She couldn't remember the last time she'd kissed a man, and even so, she'd never been kissed with the focus, the sense that the world had dropped away around them.

Her hands found the collar of his shirt and she tightened her fists into it and held on, moving her mouth under his, tasting the seltzer water on his lips. He was so very strong as he wrapped his arms around her upper arms and—

Pushed her away?

"Oh . . ." He held up his hand as if stopping something. " "Oh . . .no. Oh . . . Ronie. Shoot!" He turned away from her, wound his hand behind his neck, stepped out into the street.

And here is the final kiss of the previous LIS, *Point of No Return*:

She looked so beautiful, a smile playing on her face, her red hair down, tumbling around her shoulders. He wrapped his hand around her neck, pulled her close.

"Chet, you're hurt."

"Not that hurt."

Then he kissed her, and she was so gentle, so sweet as she touched her lips to his, and he wanted more. Would have more.

"Marry me, Mae. In Prague or Seattle. Wherever. Because when I'm with you, I'm home."

[I hope you enjoyed all that kissing. I know I did. ☺]

INGREDIENT 8: THE BREAKUP (THE REOPENING OF THE WOUND)

Don't take your love away from me . . .

If you know story structure, you know that every book must have a Black Moment. It's that moment when the hero's or heroine's greatest fears come true, and the Lie they believe feels real (the culmination of the External and Internal Obstacles.)

[To learn the basics of story structure, you may want to pick up *From the Inside . . . Out: discover, create and publish the novel in you*, the foundational guide on storycrafting.]

However, the Black Moment in romance is different than the **Breakup.** The Breakup can happen right before the Black Moment, and even contribute to the Black Moment. Or it might happen right after the Black Moment, as a *result* of the Black Moment. It might also happen all at the same time.

Let's take a look at some of our favorite Breakups:

The Pre-Black Moment Breakups:

A Walk in the Clouds: Paul and Victoria break up. He returns to reason with Victoria's father and accidently burns down the entire farm.

***Sleepless in Seattle*:** Although they aren't dating, Sam and Annie "break up" when Annie sees him with another woman after she's flown to Seattle. (The woman turns out to be his sister.) The Black Moment is when Sam's son goes missing.

Post Black Moment Breakups:

***Dirty Dancing*:** The Black Moment happens when Johnny is accused of stealing the wallet. Then he and Baby break up when he leaves.

Return to Me: Grace finds the letter and realizes that Bob's wife has her heart. This leads to their breakup.

While You Were Sleeping: Lucy confesses the truth about her relationship with Peter: that they aren't engaged, and then she waits for Jack to save her. He doesn't.

How to Lose a Guy in 10 Days: Andie discovers the bet after she's fallen for Ben—but before they break up (so eloquently and publically accomplished through the song, "You're So Vain.")

Simultaneous Black Moment/Breakup:

The Proposal: Although they aren't officially dating, Margaret and Andrew are in love, but break up at the altar when she reveals she coerced Andrew into marrying her. Her Black Moment is that she loses her "family"—and her ability to stay in America. He loses his family's respect, as well as his shot at being an editor.

In a romance, the Black Moment is not the worst part of the story—it's the climax of the external and internal journey. The *Breakup* is the darkest part of the story. The Black Moment is used to bring the character to that place where they recognize their fears and lies (and thus have an Epiphany) and make a change. This realization and change is what empowers them to pursue the relationship again. (We'll talk about the Epiphany in the next section.)

How do you create a powerful Breakup?

The Breakup happens when the hero's or heroine's wound is reopened (it may be one or both), and it is too painful for them to remain together. They believe that nothing can heal that wound, and they will forever be single.

In order to effectively use the wound, you need to start with **The Hint.** At the beginning of every great novel or movie, there is a hint at what a character's wound might be. He or she doesn't have to reveal the wound right away. The wound can be expressed in their history of relationships or how they treat potential romance.

As we elaborated earlier, the wound is derived by something that happened and they never want to repeat. It can be part of the dark moment in the past that shaped them, or perhaps something more recent. It might be something a friend has gone through, or it can be something they witness. However you want to inflict that wound, in the beginning of the novel, the hint of the wound must be injected into the story. It can be as easy as having the hero or heroine say, "I don't believe in marriage because people aren't meant to stay with one person their entire life." Of course, this might be the result of a bitter divorce of the character's parents are going through, something we find out later. But the hint has been dropped. Or a character might say, "I could never be with a man who . . . " and then name the trait that would kill the romance. (Of course it will be a trait the hero must have.) Again, there will be a dark moment reason for this statement, something in the heroine's past, but for now, we just have a hint of it.

This hint gives us a foreboding, something to recognize as the romance is played out. And, it gives resonance to the "story of the wound" the hero or heroine will tell each other. Finally, the Breakup then makes sense because we already know about the wound. (You've read those books where the hero and heroine break up and we don't know why. It turns the entire romance into a formula to be followed instead of a natural reaction to real hurt. The author hasn't hinted at the wound to prepare the reader for the Breakup.) This is why romances have a bad name!

Here are some *hints* from our favorite Matthew McConaughey movies:

In ***How to Lose a Guy in 10 days***, the heroine finds her friend crying, overwhelmed with a breakup, and we know that the heroine never wants to truly give her heart away.

In ***Fool's Gold***, the hero shows up late for his own divorce, and gets into a fight with his ex-wife about how irresponsible he is.

In ***Ghosts of Girlfriends Past***, the hero breaks up with three ladies at a time via an internet video chat. We know something is wrong with this guy.

After the hint is dropped, the next step to creating a powerful Breakup is the **Set Up.**

This is a more overt hint, even a statement of impending doom. Someone actually says, "Why are you with this guy? He'll only hurt you." Or someone says, "You always said you would never fall in love." And then that someone states the reason why. It's a step in the journey where the hero or heroine gets a small reality check of what is happening. Most of the time, they breeze right through it until the bitter Breakup. However, the Set Up confronts the possibility that the Breakup—or true love—could happen, and how the hero might react to it.

It also takes away that element of, "didn't they see that coming? Oh, they're too stupid to live." Yes, they did see it coming, but they dismissed it! It makes the story believable.

This is eloquently accomplished in *Return to Me* when Grace has a conversation with her best friend about the thank you letter she is carrying around in her pocket. They talk about the impact the letter might have on someone, and whether a person might want to know whose life the donor heart saved. We know from the conversation that Grace doesn't want to inadvertently inflict more pain on the donor family. In the end, this is exactly what she does.

We need to know that the Breakup and reopening of the wound is possible. So having someone acknowledge it in some way is a key element to building it.

So, you must *hint* and then *set it up*. You may even choose to combine them. But at some point we need to understand why they would break up.

Then, of course, we have the **Breakup.**

The Breakup occurs when the hero or heroine reopen the other's wound. Perhaps they abandon them in a time of need. Or they point out their flaw, and it's insurmountable. Or their fears of rejection push them away from the one they love. Whatever their wound is, something happens to make it so raw that they run from the relationship.

In *While you Were Sleeping*, Lucy stands at the altar and silently begs Jack to tell his family that he loves her. When he doesn't, she must stand alone and tell them the truth. Her wound is that she is alone, that she has no one, and Jack just confirmed it.

In *Return to Me*, Grace discovers the letter she wrote to Bob, and leaves. When he tracks her down and confronts her, she tells him the truth. Just as she fears, the pain of this discovery is too much and he walks out of her life.

In *Dirty Dancing*, Johnny Castle believes he's trash, and although Baby has stood up for him, he is fired. Just as he told her in the beginning, their worlds are too different for Baby and Johnny to be together, and he leaves.

Reopen the wound and it will drive them apart. It will break them up.

The Breakup needs to be clear, and it needs to happen near the end of the story. However, there needs to be enough room for hero and heroine to experience their Black Moments, their Epiphanies, and then make the grand gestures or sacrifices to win back their true love.
Give us enough time—usually three chapters before the end—to really understand the result of the Breakup. A Breakup that happens too close to the end of a book doesn't give enough room for the character change that happens as a result of it. Likewise, the Breakup can't happen too soon, or there isn't enough tension at the end of story.

After the Breakup, ideally, the hero and heroine should have a friend with whom they process the Breakup, as well as an opportunity to live life without their true love (to give us a glimpse at how terrible it is). Often there is an **"I wish I never . . ."** conversation. This is where your character regrets his or her decisions. Maybe they regret the relationship. Maybe they regret breaking up. Whatever the regret, the character takes a look at their flaws and doesn't know how to fix them. Or perhaps they don't even see their flaw. Remember, however, every flaw is based on some fear. Therefore, the Black Moment, or realization of their greatest fears, is used to help them see their flaws. This moment is key because the reader needs the character to see that they must become a better person in the journey. It's a moment of self-evaluation that gives your character the vision to go forward.

Just a note about the Black Moment: Every Black Moment has two parts. An *event*, which is the actual fear coming true, and an *effect*, which is the following emotional and spiritual crisis.

When you're constructing the Breakup, **ask: What can the hero or heroine say or do that reopens the other's wound?**

What happens next? Will you leave your character in this wounded, brokenhearted place?

No. They need to change. And get the girl. Or the guy.

Ingredient 9: The Big Why (Let's Makeup)

Instead of breakin' up I wish we were makin' up again . . .

Making up is the best part of the romance. Without a Breakup and a Makeup, we aren't sure these two will last. What if trouble comes their way? With a Breakup and a real Makeup we know they'll work through their problems and survive. A Breakup gives the characters (and the readers) a chance to step back and then to confirm their love for each other when the "Why" of their relationship is just too big to ignore.

Just to reiterate, without the Black Moment, there is no point to the journey of our character, no moment of change. It's in the Black Moment that they discover why they've gone on this journey. And it's the Black Moment—and the subsequent Epiphany—that gives them the power to make up.

So, let's take a look at the Epiphany, and then the Big Why that leads to the Makeup.

In a romance, when our hero and heroine lose the one they love and realize they can't live without them, they understand they must change in order to get what they want. Often, however, they don't know how to change. The answer lies in the Epiphany. During the Breakup and Black Moment, their flaws and fears combine to reveal some truth. Perhaps they've spent their entire life alone not because they are unlovable, but because they've always pushed people out of their lives. Maybe they can't love because they haven't forgiven the one person who hurt them. What if they are broken by the way they see themselves, or a lie they've told themselves?

In *Return to Me*, Grace believes that she shouldn't be with Bob because she'll just inflict more pain on him; she'll be a constant reminder of what he lost. But Bob tracks her down in Italy and tells her that his wife's heart rightly belongs to Grace. (And then she lets him listen to it, healing both their wounds.)

In Ghosts of Girlfriends Past, Connor Mead, the hero, listened to the lies his uncle told him about love. Since his parents were dead, he believed him. Until, through the construct of the plot, he realizes that his parents loved each other. Conner's view of relationships is skewed by his uncle's shallow view of life. He realizes that he had something real with the girl of his past—and he can have it again if he is willing to commit to her.

In order to overcome their issues, the hero and heroine must see the Lie behind their flaws and fears, embrace the Truth, and want to change.

But, in order to convince both of them that they need to change, they need to be convinced again of the **Big Why**. Returning to the wooing section, the hero and heroine gather up all the pieces of why they love each other and—usually with the help of a —friend—summarize why they love the other person. It can be a list of reasons, or one big one that shows them the essence of the one they love. It is often an expression of the core values, but it also can be how they complete each other, or make them into better people. Whatever the strongest element might be, this Big Why needs to be restated, and used as fuel to propel your hero and heroine into the next big step: The Big Gesture or Sacrifice.

Epiphany construction starts with the dark moment in the past. Remember, wounds are often based on flaws, which are often based on fears. For example, if a hero's wound is that his father left him as a child, then his flaw may be that he also leaves when someone gets too close, because his fear is being rejected again. The dark moment also produces the Lie. In this case, it may be that "if you love someone, they will leave you." Thus, his Epiphany is that love stays. Love commits. Love endures. This Truth allows him to break free of the past and pursue the relationship again.

We'll walk through this again as we construct our character in the next section, but as you're exploring the Epiphany **ask: What dark moment in the past conspired to teach your character a Lie? What Truth can set your character free?**

Ingredient 10: The Grand Gesture or Sacrifice (The wound healed)

And the Happily Ever After!

Can't buy me love!

What will it take to woo back the girl? To make the guy take your call? A broken heart isn't easily healed, and it's going to take something big to break through those newly constructed walls. I prefer to have the man pursue the woman first, but in a great romance both the hero and the heroine must confront their wounds, go through the Black Moment, have an Epiphany, and make a Grand Gesture or Sacrifice to prove their love. Whether it's declaring their love for the hero on a crowded tourist bus, or travelling half-way across the world and standing on a Paris street in the rain . . . whatever it takes to break down those walls, heal the wound, and prove that they've changed.

This is what the Big Gesture or Sacrifice is truly about. Yes, the hero or heroine wants to win back the one they love, but the story isn't just about romance. It's about how these two people met, fell in love and, as a result, changed each other for the good. Forever. We want the hero and heroine to get together and live Happily Ever After, and if they haven't solved their problems, and their deepest wounds aren't healed, then it doesn't matter how wonderful the kiss is. After the credits, they will return to their darkness.

We've talked about the construction of the wound earlier. *How do you heal it?*

Healing is accomplished in two steps:

1. The hero and heroine have to prove they have the capacity to heal the wound (usually without the other person's knowledge) during the course of the story *before the Breakup.*

Some small healing gestures from our favorite movies:

***Return to Me*:** The heroine's wound is that she has always felt vulnerable and even broken because of her bad heart. When the hero first sees the heroine filling a bottle of water with tap water, he protects her, not "exposing" her. Then, when he goes to kiss her (after one of their first dates), and she covers up her shirt (afraid he'll see her scars), he doesn't press her, again protecting her. And, when she says she had surgery, he is appropriately worried for her. He accepts her and makes her feel safe. When he arrives in Italy, he heals the wound by cherishing the heart inside her.

***You've Got Mail*:** The heroine's wound is that she hasn't found a man fully committed to her cause. Her current boyfriend is just a little too self-absorbed. The hero, however, is always encouraging. He tells her how to fight the bad guy (ironically, himself). He also loves New York, just like she does. And he reads and discusses her favorite story. It's these little tidbits that tell her that he can heal her wounds of losing something she held so dear.

Drop these healing moments into the story. Combine them with the Why moments. But having them intact in their past allows the hero and heroine to recognize them during the Make up.

2. The second step is The Grand Gesture, or the healing that comes with the hero's or heroine's Sacrificial Gesture. This must be something big that they can surrender in order to heal the wound of the other.

The Grand Gesture or Sacrifice convinces the reader that your hero or heroine is truly a changed person. They will use to make their Grand Gesture or Sacrifice that heals the wound of the one they love. In this moment, give your hero or heroine something they must do. It must be a proactive event that will challenge their truth, but give them an opportunity to prove their love. Maybe it's a confrontation, or a declaration, or a surrender, or a challenge--whatever it might be, it has to be something that will test their heart.

Often, the person with the biggest wound makes a small gesture as a way of healing, but the other then reaches out with a Grand Gesture or Sacrifice that completes it. Or, you can have the Grand Gesture started by the stronger of the two (we love it when it's the hero, but it can also be the heroine). It's then returned by the other. Regardless, it must be accomplished by both parties.

For example, in a recent movie, *Leap Year,* the heroine's wound is that no man wants to build a life with her. (Her fiancé actually asks her to marry him so they'll get this great apartment.) The hero's wound is that he invested in a woman who ran off with someone else (rejection). The heroine finally gathers up the nerve to return to Ireland where she proposes to the hero. He says nothing and she thinks that he has rejected her and leaves. The hero, however, chases her down the shore with a ring. He does want to build a life with her.

The Grand Gesture is all about the hero or heroine recognizing (or at least the author recognizing) the deep wound in the other, and healing it with a sacrificial (or vulnerable) act. It's when they lay out their heart for the other.

Let's return to *Dirty Dancing,* a classic Grand Gesture ending.

Baby is sitting in the corner at her parents' table when Johnny roars in. He goes right up to her father, who stands to protect her, and says, "Nobody puts Baby in the corner." Meaning, it's time for Baby to grow up. Then he gives his record to a friend and goes to the middle of the stage and tells the truth: That he always ends the season with a dance, but that this year, someone told him not to. But he'd learned, through the example of Baby (whom he calls Frances) that when you believe in someone or something, you stand up for it. So, he's arrived to dance the last dance to his kind of music with his partner, Baby.

Another Grand Gesture is Jack, in *While You Were Sleeping,* arriving at the subway toll booth with his family to propose to Lucy.

A Sacrifice is when Paul, in *A Walk in the Clouds,* humbles himself before Victoria's father at the winery to convince him of his honor, and then he nearly loses his life as he fights to save the vineyard.

A Sacrifice is Andie giving up her magazine job in D.C. to stay in New York to be with Ben in *How to Lose a Guy in 10 Days.* (And his corresponding Grand Gesture is chasing her down in her cab when she is on the way to the airport.)

The Grand Gesture or Sacrifice proves the hero and heroine have changed, and are willing to do anything to win back the heart of the one they love. It's most often the finale of the romance, right before they live happily ever after.

One way to plot this moment is to **ask: What would you never sacrifice, or what would you never do for love?**

Another way to look at it is to **ask: What can the hero or heroine do that heals the wound for the other?**

The healing of the wound is the *key* to a Happily Ever After (HEA) ending.

How do you use this Grand Gesture or Sacrifice to craft the HEA ending?

The HEA ending is one part wound healing, one part Greatest Dream. Just like when you explore the dark moment of your character's past and you use the answers to build the break up and Black Moment and Epiphany, you also need to examine the hero's and the heroine's past for their happiest moment. We ask this because we want to find that one moment when everything worked, everything was right. We want to extrapolate from that some element that we can then use in the ending.

Consider the ending in *Return to Me*: The greatest dream for the hero, of course, is to have his wife back. (His happiest moment being epitomized right before she died, at the dance.) But, we know he'll never have that. But, he does have a piece if her—and even better, his wife has almost "blessed" his relationship with Gracie. Gracie's greatest dream (her happiest moment was when she got her new heart) is to thank the person who gave her the heart, and to live a good life. (She feels a little guilty that someone had to die to give her life). To be able to "give" the hero a little something of his wife, and know that she makes him happy too, is a fulfillment of her greatest dream,
The HEA ending is a combination of healing the wound (for Gracie, being accepted despite the cost, and for the hero, allowing himself to love again), and the greatest dream.

How to find this?

1. Determine the wound. What would heal this?
2. Determine the greatest dream. What part of this can you (as the author) give them?

It's Johnny and Baby dancing with the staff and the resort guests, all enjoying the same music at the end of *Dirty Dancing*. (This event heals Johnny's "bad boy" self-image and Baby's betrayal by her father, giving them both an affirmation that they changed "the world" through dancing.)

It's Victoria's father telling her to teach her husband how to plant a vineyard in *A Walk through the Clouds*. (This heals her wound of shame, and his wound of abandonment, and gives them both a heritage, together).

It's Jack putting a stamp in Lucy's passport (in *While You Were Sleeping*) and giving her the world.

Plot the Breakup

What is the hero's wound?

What is the heroine's wound?

What can the hero or heroine say or do that reopens the other's wound?

Hero:

Heroine:

Plot the Epiphany

What lie does your hero believe? What Truth sets him free?

What lie does your heroine believe? What Truth sets her free?

Build the Happily Ever After

Part One: Heal the Wound

What would your hero never sacrifice, or what would he never do for love?

What would your heroine never sacrifice, or what would she never do for love?

What can the hero or heroine do that heals the wound for the other?

Hero:

Heroine:

Part Two: Give them their Greatest Dream:

- ✓ What is your heroine's happiest moment in her past?

- ✓ What is her Greatest Dream?

- ✓ How will she find a piece of this Greatest Dream in the HEA?

- ✓ What is your hero's happiest moment in his past?

- ✓ What is his Greatest Dream?

- ✓ How will he find a piece of this Greatest Dream in the HEA?

SECTION TWO

BUILDING THE PERFECT ROMANCE HERO AND HEROINE

Worksheets

Although you have taken time to think through the questions that help you build the ingredients of your novel in Section One, now that you understand how the ingredients work together, fill and hone the elements in the work text questions below. As the ingredients become richer, the story will take on power and resonance and come to life as you deepen each area. In Section Three, I'll show you how to apply these ingredients into the Three Act Story Structure.

Who is your hero?

Basic Bio:

Name:

Age:

Profession:

Tell me about yourself:

Who are you? (**Identity**) How do you express this identity through your appearance?

What sort of behaviors, mannerisms, and trappings go along with that identity?

What monumental event in your past shaped you? Journal it—with details. (Tell the story.)

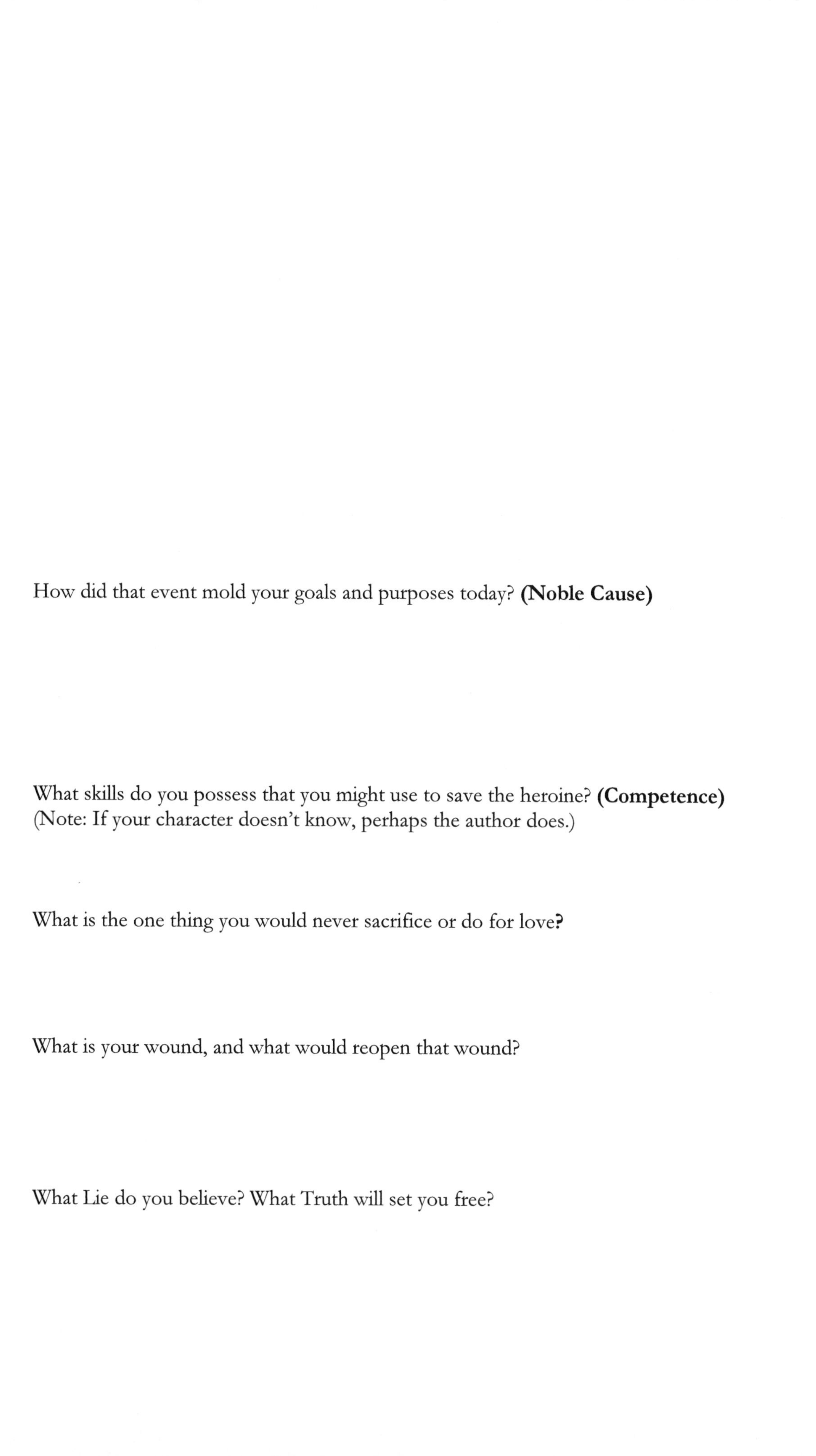

How did that event mold your goals and purposes today? **(Noble Cause)**

What skills do you possess that you might use to save the heroine? **(Competence)**
(Note: If your character doesn't know, perhaps the author does.)

What is the one thing you would never sacrifice or do for love?

What is your wound, and what would reopen that wound?

What Lie do you believe? What Truth will set you free?

What is the happiest moment in your past? (This helps you, the author, determine what they want.)

Why do you think you'll never get it? (**Obstacles**)

Remember: Backstory Breadcrumbs are soft, tasty, *small* morsels that lure your reader into the story.

In the beginning**, w**hat is the *essential* information the reader needs to know to give sufficient motivation for the character?

Who is your heroine?

Basic Bio:

Name:

Age:

Profession:

Tell me about yourself:

Who are you? (**Identity**) How do you express this identity through your appearance?

What sort of behaviors, mannerisms, and trappings go along with that identity?

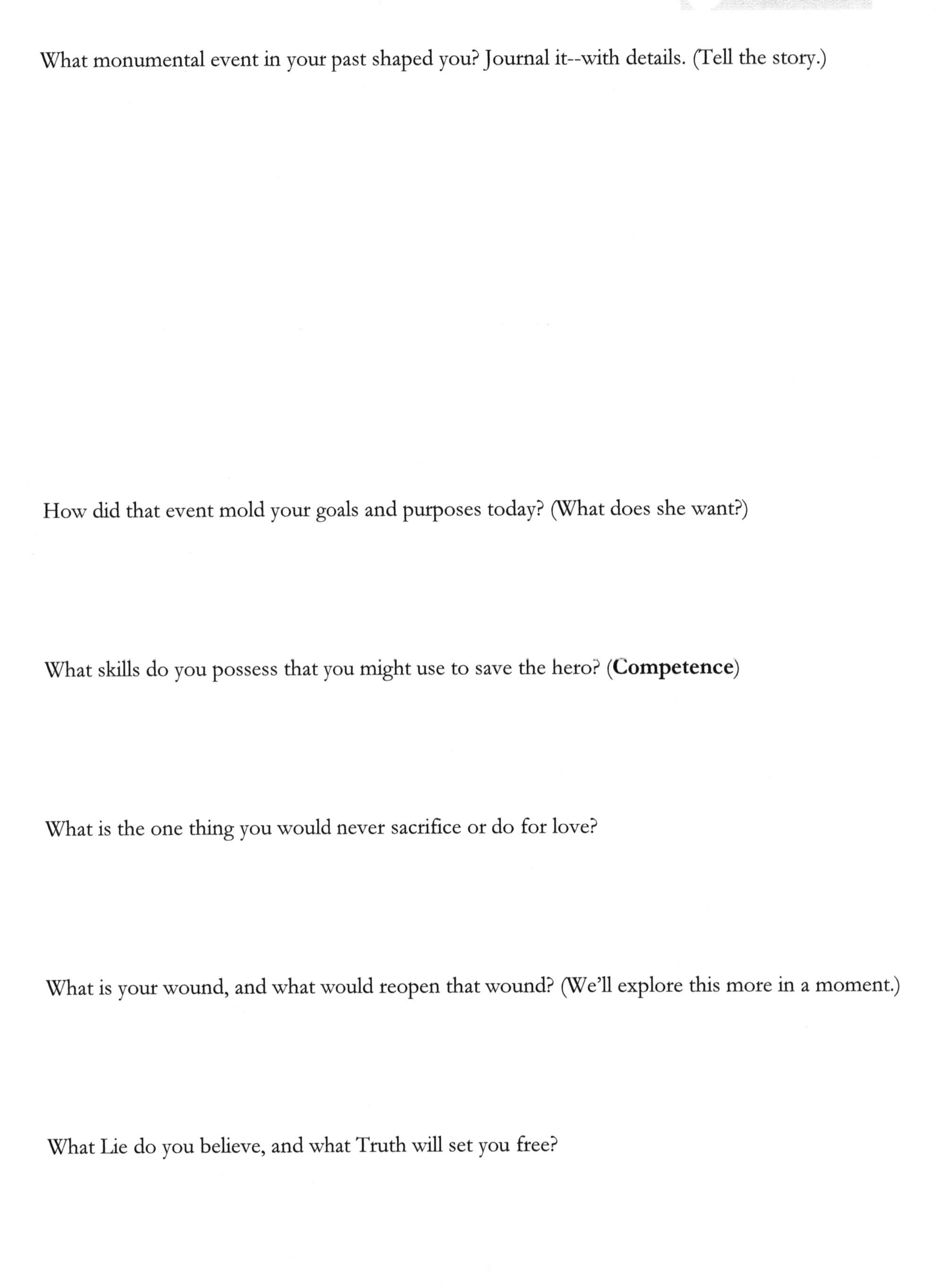

What monumental event in your past shaped you? Journal it--with details. (Tell the story.)

How did that event mold your goals and purposes today? (What does she want?)

What skills do you possess that you might use to save the hero? (**Competence**)

What is the one thing you would never sacrifice or do for love?

What is your wound, and what would reopen that wound? (We'll explore this more in a moment.)

What Lie do you believe, and what Truth will set you free?

What is the happiest moment in your past? (This helps you determine what they want.)

Why do you think you'll never get it? (**Obstacles**)

In the beginning, what is the *essential* information the reader needs to know to give sufficient motivation for the character?

Developing the key ingredients

Boy Meets Girl

Build Your Hero:

Reminder of his Noble Cause:

- ✓ What underlying cause are you "fighting for" that makes us love you?

Make him likeable:

- ✓ What sweet, kind, and sacrificial "Boy Scout" moment can you insert into the story early on to stir the readers' love for the hero?

Find his Flaw and Fear:

- ✓ Why did your last girlfriend break up with you? Or: Why haven't you found true love?

- ✓ What is the fear behind the flaw?

Give him Courage:

- ✓ What will you do that shows your courage to change in order to get the girl?

Build your Heroine:

Reiterate her Goal:

- ✓ What do you want?

Find her Flaw and Fear:

- ✓ What is your biggest flaw?

- ✓ Why? What fear drives this flaw?

Build her Confidence:

- ✓ What are you good at, and how does that skill help save the day?

- ✓ What can you do at the end of the book that you couldn't do at the beginning?

Make her Beautiful:

- ✓ How does your heroine complement or balance the hero?

- ✓ What does your heroine do that affirms the hero? How does she accentuate his strengths?

- ✓ How is your heroine irresistible to the hero? (Ask the hero: What draws you to her? Why can't you live without her?)

Interest and Need

Build the Meeting:

Ask the Hero:

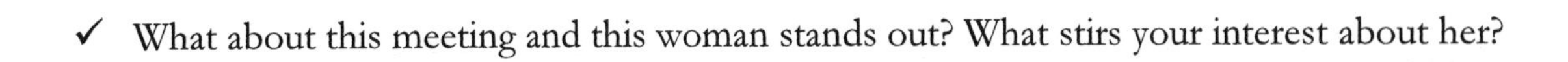

- ✓ What about this meeting and this woman stands out? What stirs your interest about her?

- ✓ Why would you like to fall in love?

Ask the Heroine:

- ✓ What about this meeting and this man stands out? What stirs your interest about him?

- ✓ Why would you like to fall in love?

Building the Romance Whys

- A hero and heroine complete each other.
- The hero and heroine make each other better people.
- The hero and heroine share essential values.

Ask the Hero:

✓ What can the heroine do for you that you can't do yourself?

✓ How does she affirm you? How does she accentuate your strength? How do you become a better person when you are together?

✓ What core values do you share?

Ask the Heroine:

✓ What can the hero do for you that you can't do yourself?

✓ How does he affirm you? How does he accentuate your strength? How do you become a better person when you are together?

✓ What core values do you share?

As you build your characters, you want to look at their inadequacies and see how they complete each other. In the chart below write the name of your hero at the top of one column, and the name of your heroine in the other.

When you are building your story, you'll want to build in moments and scenes where readers see them building their romance. Brainstorm some *Why* scenes for each element.

Scenes	Hero	Heroine
They complete each other		
They better each other		
They share core values		

Why Not?

Building the plot Why Nots: (The External Obstacles)
What realistic, External Obstacle in the plot pushes your hero and heroine apart?

When you're building your romance, sometimes it helps to make a chart, putting the hero on one side, the heroine on the other, and comparing and contrasting their Noble Cause and Goals. It's a great way to find those External Obstacles that keep them apart.

	Hero	Heroine
Noble Cause/Goal		
External Obstacles		

Building the Internal Why Nots (and the Wound)

Ask your Hero:

- ✓ What is the worst thing that ever happened to you (preferably romantically, but it can be anything that involves the heart). What wound did it leave?

- ✓ How has that affected your past relationships?

Ask your Heroine:

- ✓ What is the worst thing that ever happened to you (preferably romantically, but it can be anything that involves the heart). What wound did it leave?

- ✓ How has that affected your past relationships?

A look at your story Arc:

Is it a Why/Why Not or a Why Not/Why?

Constructing the Breakup:

- ✓ What can the hero say or do that reopens the wound of the heroine?

- ✓ What can the heroine say or do that reopens the wound of the hero?

- ✓ What event makes your hero and heroine break up?

Add in the Black Moment:

- ✓ What is your hero's greatest fear?

- ✓ What is your heroine's greatest fear?

- ✓ How do these greatest fears come true in a Black Moment Event?

Black Moment - Hero:

Black Moment - Heroine:

Exploration of the Epiphany:

- ✓ What Truth sets the Hero free?

- ✓ What Truth sets the Heroine free?

Grand Gesture and Sacrifice:

- ✓ What can the hero do that heals the heroine's wound?

- ✓ What can the heroine do that heals the hero's wound?

Finding the Happily Ever After:

- ✓ What is your hero's happiest moment from the past? How can you reconstruct this or give them a taste of this in the future?

- ✓ What is your heroine's happiest moment? How can you reconstruct this or give them a taste of this in the future?

Section 3

Putting it all together

Adding the Ingredients into your Story Structure

You've built your hero and heroine, gathered all the ingredients . . . now it's time to insert them into your story arc and build your romance. Just as a recap, remember every genre book has key elements—things we expect from that genre novel. A suspense has a ticking time bomb and a deadline. A mystery has a dead body and red herrings. A romance also has the ten ingredients that we expect. However, the author has license to change up these elements, putting them in a different order.

And of course, the author brings his or her own voice to the romance—telling it in a way only her or she knows how. That is why we watch remakes of old films. Even though it is the same story, it has a different take, and we love that. We love seeing the new voice on the old structure!

Now that we know the ten ingredients, we are armed to put it together in our own unique way. Here's the secret trick -- identifying these ten ingredients makes writing your synopsis *sooooo* easy. At least, it makes writing the framework easy, because you know the basic elements that craft a romance.

Most of all, they ensure that your romance has all the appropriate beats to make it satisfying. Now that you know the ingredients, let's weave them into Act One.

Act 1 Application

Let's start by taking a look at the main ingredients of Act 1:

Boy Meets Girl: In this component, there is an event, goal, or circumstance that occurs to bring our hero and heroine together. Usually this happens in the first chapter, but it definitely needs to happen by chapter three.

Some classic Boy Meets Girl events:

You've Got Mail -- The hero and heroine are both in a chat room and start talking about New York City in the fall.

***Sleepless in Seattle* --** The phone call to the radio show causes the hero and heroine to "meet" over the radio.

***While You Were Sleeping* --** The hero and heroine meet at Christmas at the family's home.

***The Cutting Edge* --** The hero and heroine bump into each other at the Olympics when he knocks her down. But they really meet later, when she needs a skating partner.

***Titanic* --** The hero and heroine meet on the ship.

***Chasing Liberty* --** The heroine runs out of a concert and needs a ride to get away from the paparazzi.

***Return to Me* --** The hero meets the heroine while on a bad date in the restaurant.

As you sketch out your novel, you start by defining that Boy Meets Girl moment. Give it a sentence or two.

Here's my Boy Meets Girl moment from my Love Inspired Suspense, *Undercover Pursuit.*

Boy Meets Girl: They're both there for different weddings at the same location. They get into the same cab, mistaking each other for people they haven't met—but are supposed to.

(And since you don't know what is in my head, here's some info you might need: The hero is undercover, supposed to meet up with another agent. He will pose as her fiancé and protect the bride. The heroine is supposed to be the maid of honor at her sister's wedding—and the blind date of one of the groomsmen.)

Once you have your Boy Meets Girl moment, you can move on to the next ingredient:

Interest and Need: Something about their own situation makes their heart vulnerable to romance.

Let's look at some of the movies mentioned:

Titanic -- Rose hates her life, feels suffocated, and longs for freedom and adventure. Jack is a vagabond, and when he sees this beautiful woman who loves him, he is affirmed. She believes in him!

Sleepless in Seattle -- Annie is marrying a man she doesn't really love. Sam lost the only woman he thinks he can ever love.

It's very important for you to figure out what it is about your characters that make them ready or vulnerable to romance. Often this element is revealed though a conversation they have with their friends. Or it is a part of Inciting Incident.

Or it is played out through the actions. In my book *Nothing But Trouble*, my heroine, PJ Sugar, breaks up with her beau during the first scene. She wants a man who can see past her tattoos to the real girl.

Here's an example from my LIS novel, *Undercover Pursuit:*

Interest and Need –

The heroine's sister is marrying the man that she thought liked her. She is tired of living outside the romance novel.

The hero used to be a wild guy and has changed his ways. Now he's afraid to be with a woman because he doesn't know how to date a nice girl. But he wants someone he can love and trust, and someone who sees him as a hero.

What makes your character vulnerable to love?
Right now, you're just building the components. Remember, you can move them around to fit the story.

(We're going to skip over the Why right now (but we'll be coming back to it) and move onto the next beat:)

Why Not: These are the obstacles between the hero and heroine that conspire to separate them.

Remember, we analyzed two different structures: Why/Why Not and Why Not/Why.

The Why Not/Why romance structure is when the obstacles appear first and the Why appears second to pull them together.

Or you may have a Why/Why Not structure where they fall in love first and then realize why they can't be together. A hint of the obstacles in the beginning are a way to keep the tension high between them even in a Why/Why Not story.

Here are the Why Nots for *Undercover Pursuit*: He needs her to be his date to accomplish the mission he is on. She feels like he tricked her—and now trapped her—into helping him. They don't trust each other.

So, now we have the three ingredients we'll be using to insert into our Act One elements.

(Note: If you are not familiar with basic story structure, refer to Appendix 1 for reference. You may also want to pick up a copy of *From the Inside . . . Out: discover, create and publish the novel in you*!)

Let's review Act One:

ACT ONE APPLICATION

Act One
Life
Inciting Incident
The Big Debate
Noble Quest

We start with **Life**—that snapshot of their ordinary, everyday world, aka the starting place of their journey. Many romances start with the hero and heroine meeting in the **Life** scene or chapter. If you are writing for Love Inspired or Heartsong, this is a must. If you are writing a longer trade novel, you can have them meet in chapter two, but definitely, you want them together by chapter three.

So, let's say you're putting them together in chapter one. Along with the other first chapter elements of hinting at what is at **Stake** for your character, putting them in a **Sympathetic Situation** (or a situation that makes the reader identify with them), **Anchoring** them into the story world, starting with the story already in motion and finally hinting at the story problem, you also want to weave in the ingredients:

Boy Meets Girl – You want them to meet each other. They don't have to talk to each other, but you want to make a statement that they've seen each other. Some of my first scenes are running into each other, seeing one or the other on television, tracking someone down as the object of an investigation, being assigned to protect or interview or fire someone. Asking for a job, rescuing someone on the side of the road, being assigned to work with them—anything that would put them together. They might even be haggling over the same pumpkin or Christmas tree! Whatever works. Like I said, they don't have to talk. They just have to remember meeting each other.

Start with asking: How do your characters meet?

Weave their meeting in with the other chapter one elements. Can you combine this with creating character **Sympathy**? For example, in *Escape to Morning*, my heroine has just come off a body recover with her K9 SAR dog, and the hero nearly runs the dog over with his car. He feels badly for her, so he invites her out for dinner.

After you have the **Boy Meets Girl**, you might add in an **Interest** or a **Need.** Something about their life suggests they are single, or in need of a good woman (or man). For example, in *Taming Rafe* my heroine has a date to her gala event, but he's rude and condescending and it is clear she's with the wrong man. In *Nothing but Trouble*, my heroine, PJ, breaks up with her boyfriend in the first scene and thoughts of her old beau Boone enter her mind almost immediately. (This is how I get him on the page. ☺)

In Reclaiming Nick, Piper sees Nick as a patron of his café, and watches him rescue a girl in need. She makes a comment about how she doesn't need a man rescuing her. We realize she's never had anyone protect her.

They may not *realize* they have a need or interest, but the reader does by the way they react, the comments they make, or an opinion, or internal thought. Remember, the key of this scene is that the characters notice each other. Something about them piques their interest because they have a need or latent desire for a relationship.

Ask: How do your characters show they have an interest or need for romance?

Finally, you're going to add in tension by hinting at the Why Not. Let's go back to the other elements. You might incorporate the element of **Sympathy** here. Or you could move onto the **Stakes** of the story: What might happen if she doesn't get what she wants, and how does he stand in the way of it? Let the Why Not do double duty and be a part of her overall conflict.

For example, in *Reclaiming Nick*, Piper's and Nick's Why Not is that she is trying to prove that he helped kill her brother. At stake is her career. She's trying to land an anchor position and getting this story will cinch it. If she proves his guilt, then she gets the job. The Why Not plays a role in the plot. She has to choose between happily ever after in love, or happily ever after in her job.

Again, just to reiterate, early in the first three chapters, you must establish their home world. Have your characters meet in a way that helps the reader feel sympathy for your characters and also show that they have an interest or need for something more, namely, a romance. You must hint at the stakes of the story, and weave that in with the Why Not (or obstacles) between your characters. Maybe your heroine says, "The last person she wanted in her life was a know-it-all redneck," right before her car breaks down in the middle of the northern Minnesotan woods, where a very buff logger redneck walks out of the forest to help her get back on the road. ☺

So, let's move the romance thread a bit further along, using our Why/Why Nots to help jump start the romance.

The Inciting Incident should cause a need to arise in the hero and heroine—so much so that they are "invited" by either an external or internal force to go on a "journey" or Noble Quest. Although this is a plot element, likewise, they are going on a romantic journey as well. They may decide not to pursue the object of their affection at the moment, but you are going to feed the internal interest or needs by giving them a glimpse of one of the Whys. By doing this, you will lower their defenses for a second meeting.

Now, pick one of the Why elements and insert a hint of it in Act One, as a sort of "pull" toward each other. Can they observe the other doing something that speaks to their values? Can the hero do something for the heroine that she can't do, or vice versa? Or are they briefly working together or challenging each other to become better people?

Think about Act One of your favorite romances: What *Why* do the hero and heroine hint at even before they begin their wooing or relationship?

For example, in *Return to Me*, the hero sees the heroine filling up the water bottle of the crabby patron in the sink. This act feeds his internal values. He likes down to earth people. When he doesn't rat her out to his date, this ignites her interest and need for a man who might accept her (which, ultimately, is her hope). Thus, she writes him a little note in his take-out meal. Likewise, he hopes to see her when he goes back for his phone . . . and the story continues from there.

Of course, there must also be something holding them apart, or it would be love at first sight. Which means we need to return to the Why Nots. What obstacles have you put before your hero and heroine? If you are constructing a Why Not/Why romance structure, then the Why Nots at the beginning should be looming. There should not be a doubt in the hero's and heroine's minds that this is *not* the one. This makes that hint of Why ever more important. They have to have a smidge of an impulse to connect with the other again.

If you are constructing a Why/Why Not romance, then the Whys will be large and beautiful, and you'll need to hint at the Why Not, a blip of why things might go wrong.

Return to Me is a Why/Why Not romance because from the hero's and heroine's POVs, they have no obstacles until the big Why Not at the end. So, the Whys seem glorious and beautiful until they begin to get closer and she might have to tell him about her surgery. And then, the Why Nots are devastating when she has to tell him the truth about the origin of her heart. But, the first hints of the Why Nots are when they are on their first date and she is telling him about her dreams and riding her bike and why this is so wonderful. She can't really tell him why, can she? The author has hinted at the Why Not to come.

I know it's a lot to think about. And yes, you can stretch some of these elements over the first couple chapters. But as you put together your romance, you need to know how to let elements do double-duty and lay a firm foundation for every story thread.

These three ingredients comprise the bulk of Act One.

ACT TWO APPLICATION

By the time you enter into Act Two, you should have already accomplished setting up your character's home world, thrown in the Inciting Incident combined in some way with hero and heroine meeting as well as hinted at the Why/Why Not. If you don't have that firm foundation of your characters' wants, their fears, their Whys/Why Nots of the romance and their lies, then you aren't ready to move into Act Two.

If you are putting the ingredients into standard Story Structure, it might look like this: (Again, refer to the Appendix)

ACT Two (Fun and Games!)

- Disappointments
  - Y in the Road
- Destruction)
  - Y in the Road
- Devastation (and the transition to Act 3)

If you've taken the time to build this for your character, then you're ready for the fun part of the book: the **Sparks** and the **Wooing**, as well as **Sexual Tension** (the Kiss!). We're building tension and romance in order to create the Breakup and Black Moment at the end of Act Two.

Let's take a look at the ingredients:

Wooing

This is the fun stuff—all those "dates" or events they have that make them fall for each other. Just as a reminder, what are some of the dates or wooing we've seen?

One of my favorite is in ***While you Were Sleeping*** -- Moving the sofa!
Notting Hill -- Reading lines together.

How to Lose a Guy in 10 Days -- Learning to ride the motorcycle and playing cards with his family.
The Wedding Planner -- Going to the outdoor theater and eating M&M'S
50 First Dates -- Classic dates, over and over again. Meeting the sea creatures and the waffle dates.

During wooing, it's important to pick scenes that will engage the reader, something the reader might like to do. You really can be creative with the wooing moments. I've used motorcycle rides, trips to the dump to watch the bears, a late night hockey game, an overnight car ride, a trip to the library, a snowmobile ride. Think outside the box. Where would *you* like to go?

For every romance, I try and plot at least *one* great date scene, and a couple smaller scenes. Need ideas? Look at the Whys chart. Have you plotted a scene for each of these? Whys make fabulous wooing scenes.

Sizzle!

Now remember, your goal in a romance is to draw your hero and heroine together, and cause them to fall in love (even if they don't know it), all the while honing that final Why Not to a sharp point. It's a delicate balance. Let's look at how to do this.

You do this best by creating some Spark and Sizzle.

Spark happens when two stubborn, hard objects (like flint!) that are hit together. Another way to create fire is to create tension, or friction, between two objects. With flint stone, these objects are both sharp, and the force of them colliding causes a tiny bit of rock to break off, and thus, a spark is made.

Let's apply this to our romance.
First, we need to get the hero and heroine together. It's hard to fall in love when you're not talking to each other.

This is when spark happens: Two people from two opposite viewpoints find themselves in conflict. You must have scenes where they are together and have opposite goals. Of course, as the wooing continues, their goals will become more aligned but initially, to start the flame, some sort of conflict is necessary.

Even if you are building a Why/Why Not story (with the major conflict coming after they've fallen in love), you can create conflict. For example, in my book *Nothing But Trouble*, PJ and Jeremy meet and are driven by the common goal of escaping the scene of a murder investigation (and Boone, the former boyfriend and police detective) undetected. How they do this causes conflict. Not only that, but what they do afterward is also a source of heated dialogue. They belong together, their Why is leading the romance (and the Why Not comes up at the end), but their *goals in the scene are contrary.*

So, how will you create sparks in a scene?

The best way to express this is through Dialogue. A great romance has a lot of Sizzle! I love a book or movie with great dialogue. It's that Spark between the hero and heroine that make us fall in love with them. You want to build in some witty conversation, and especially fights! A great fight causes great tension. But as we talked about in the dialogue section, you don't have to have a fight to have Sizzle.

My two favorite scenes in *While You Were Sleeping* are the couch scene and the walk home, which ends with the "leaning" scene. These scenes have great dialogue because the hero and heroine share their dark moments and greatest dreams. It's key that you allow your characters to share the dark moment. Let them actually tell us, because it not only wins the hearts of your hero and heroine, but also your readers. The sharing of the greatest dream works likewise. We begin to root for their happy ending!

But remember, the best dialogue, the most revealing dialogue, happens during a fight. Yet, how do you make the argument seem real, not contrived, and not about one being childish, or about a simple misunderstanding?

1. A fight might start with a misunderstanding (as most fights do!) but in the end, they are often about C**ore Values**.

What the hero and heroine believe about each other, or things they need to confront. A good fight should make each of them think about who they are and cause some shift toward change in their lives. (As do all good fights.) A fight built on a misunderstanding at its core is frustrating for readers. And although we'll buy it for a while, as the hero and heroine grow deeper in their relationship, it needs to be a real core issue that holds them apart.

Let's take *You've Got Mail.* The romance tension is basically built on "miscommunication." But as we go deeper, we realize that he has unraveled her entire life, and she might not forgive him once she finds out who he is. So he has to woo her in the flesh to get her to overcome the "little misunderstanding" they had about the shop, and his identity online.

Another movie is *Return to Me.* This too, is based on miscommunication. We want to say to the heroine "Just tell him already!" But when we see that the core issue is that she thinks she'll always be a reminder of his loss, then we realize it truly is an obstacle.

Get at the core of their misunderstanding and make that Why Not be the root of the argument—not the miscommunication. The biggest fight, the one that keeps them apart, should be about core values.

2. Making it real means you *weave your way into the fight.* Don't have them immediately blow up.

Peel back the layers until the characters get to the core of the fight. I also allow my characters to fight dirty. I use sarcasm and name calling. I will even throw things (all things I would never do in real life ☺). Think of the Zingers we explored in the Dialogue section.

3. Finally, don't have a huge fight on every page. Save the big fight for the climactic moment that opens the wounds, or exposes their fears.

A good fight scene reveals the core of the character . . . the issues they've been dancing around. A good fight scene really has to get straight to the core, revelatory issues. Otherwise it's boring and you lose the good stuff in between.

At the end of the core fight, your characters should be naked and bleeding. You want them to take a good look at problems and grow from them.

This is just my opinion, but polite fights (unless it is subtexting) are cheesy fights. You want them to say something really sharp, profound. Which means it might get rough out there. And most of all, no apologizing. Don't pull your punches! If she calls him a jerk, let it hang out there. Don't write that she feels bad and says "I shouldn't have said that." You might have her think later, "I shouldn't have said that," but at the time, don't. It lessens the energy of the fight. Too often a great fight, and great dialogue, loses its power because the author pulls back from that great, painful moment. If it needs to be said—say it!

So, build in a great fight—or a series of good fights and conflict between the hero and heroine, and you'll have a story with Sizzle!

Need more help? Here are some ideas as you construct Wooing and Sizzle Scenes.

First, start with their goals. **What do they need to accomplish?**

Then ask: **how can you put the other person in that scene in a way that stands in their way?** Or, if you are creating a Why/Why Not story, how can you put that person in a scene that assists them on their journey, yet still creates mini-conflict in the scene?

Another way to plot Act Two is to look at the Why Nots. How can you continue to insert these, one by one, into the story until finally they become glaring?

But Susie, don't we want them to fall in love? They can't do that if they are constantly fighting.

You're right! So after we set off the sparks, we need to kindle the fire with some more wooing. Draw them back to each other. This is the key to keeping the flame alive. You want to always be adding more kindling to the fire, but with both Whys and Why Nots. Sizzle and Wooing. For every wooing scene, follow up with a Sizzle scene. And, the more they fall in love, the more they are wooed, the greater the fear of failure when the conflict happens, because we want them to succeed!

I know I keep preaching about the Whys, but without Whys, we end a story saying, "I don't buy it. Why did those two belong together?" And we leave readers in doubt, without believing the HEA ending.

Let's bring it back to Act Two construction. You dropped in a hint of one of these Whys in Act One. Now, it's time to really go for the gusto. Create scenes that really develop these three elements. Even if you are creating a Why/Why Not, you'll want to strengthen the Why (because the Why Not will be so devastating they will need to have strong Whys to overcome it). Plot moments to build values, to complete each other and to make them into better people. The Wooing is the feeding of the fire, then the nurturing of the Sizzle.

Wooing is about making us realize, slowly, that he or she is the *One*.

So, as you are plotting and writing Act 2, ask yourself: Are they getting along too well? Is their relationship too easy? It could be time to throw in some Sizzle. But, if they are fighting too much, give them a wooing scene.

Wooing and Sizzle can also be accomplished in one fell swoop with a *Kiss*.

The Sexual Tension (the Kiss!).

We covered this earlier, but let's recap.

Kiss One: An introductory "I didn't mean to, did we just do that?" Kiss
Kiss Two: An "I really want to kiss you now and I'm going to," Kiss
Kiss Three: An "I love you, and I mean it," Kiss

If you have to save word count, the last two can be combined.

Of course, before the first kiss you, want to build desire, an awareness of each other, an agreement that they aren't repulsed by each other, and even a hope that maybe, oh, no, really, oh, I shouldn't think that but *yes*, I want to kiss him!

This progression of desire often happens before the introductory kiss. But you *can* have an intro kiss that takes them off guard, one that they then ponder later and the desire starts to build as they decide they like it. *A lot.*

Between the intro kiss and the "I really want to kiss you," kiss, there is Wooing and Sparks and some Whys, until they realize their heart is engaged. This kiss means something.

The intro kiss should occur before or at the halfway point of the book. If you were to pick up a Steeple Hill or Harlequin, you could open half way, and usually there is the kissing (okay, the sex scene). The second kiss occurs in the last quarter of the book. Usually.

Often, after that kiss we might have the Black Moment. However, the Black Moment could happen after the intro kiss and the second kiss could be combined with the last kiss.

In my current WIP, my hero and heroine are pretending to be engaged. Which causes them to be in romantic situations. They have a *fake* kiss half way through the book that leads to real attraction.

The second kiss is combined with the last kiss and occurs at the end. (Unless they absolutely demand another one! Which they might.)

As far as kissing rules: Write the kiss you are comfortable with, one you'd like to read, the one that feels real. Regardless of the amount or type of kisses you have, they should only cause more wooing, more tension, and lead them to toward the Breakup and Act Three.

ACT THREE APPLICATION

This is it. The Grand Finale. The messy Breakup, the Black Moment, the Make Up, the Grand Gesture and Sacrifice, the happy ending. Act 3 is what we've been waiting for.

Act 3 Story Structure:

HELP! Or *Climax*
Overhaul
Perfect Ending Resolution

Let's take a look at the ingredients:

The Breakup: This is when the biggest Why Not rises to push them apart. Every romance has a Breakup. That reason why they can't be together. Without it, we have no triumphant run into each other's arms! We have no giant sigh of happiness. We have no conflict, tension, and late night reading!

In *Undercover Pursuit*, my hero's mission is going to get an untrained person hurt, and he can't fall for her, so he stages a Breakup. This fight embarrasses and hurts her, and she believes all his feelings for her were just an act, which gets at her core issues that she's a "leftover."And then she does something that makes him think she can't be trusted (his Why Not). Now, their Breakup is real.

The Breakup is essential to a romance, because we want true love to win. If true love isn't at stake, then there is not fear of losing, no turning pages.

So, how do you incorporate the Breakup?

As we talked about in the Breakup chapter, the Breakup is separate from the Black Moment Event—that event that embodies their greatest fear and that causes the hero and heroine to believe their lies. Still, the Breakup is **integrally tied to the Black Moment Event.** The two affect each other.

The Breakup can either happen *before* the Black Moment Event—something that then moves the character into their Black Moment Event, e.g. they break up, and then (in a romantic suspense, for example) the villain captures the heroine and the hero (because of the Breakup) isn't around to protect her, thus leading to *his* Black Moment.

Or, it could happen *during* the Black Moment Event—using the same scenario. The hero and heroine break up while they are both being held hostage by the villain, because they realize that neither of them trusts each other. (Or some other reason.)

Or, it could happen *as a result* of the Black Moment Event—after the hero rescues her, he realizes that it is too dangerous for her to be in a relationship with someone who brings danger to her door, thus, he breaks up with her.

Wherever you put the Breakup, it needs to affect, or be affected by the Black Moment Event in some way.

After the Breakup, they're going to realize **The Great Why**.

The core reason they belong together saves the day. After their hearts are breaking, they will, realize they can't live without each other. If you've set up Act 2 correctly, the reader will see why they need to be together (because you will be showing us those essential Why scenes. But at this key moment, after the Breakup, the characters will realize why they belong together, and this reason is bigger than the Why Not of the Breakup. They will do anything to be together.

Think about this: Why should some of our heroes and heroines of our favorite movies be together?

How to Lose a Guy in 10 Days -- Ben and Andie are both competitive, but they appreciate each other.

While You Were Sleeping -- Jack understands Lucy's loyalty to her father, and her desire to see the world, and Lucy understands Jack's desire for quality.

Remember, the Whys are at the core of a person. That essential Why which is the glue that holds them together despite your misunderstandings.

Here are the Whys in my current WIP:

My hero has always wanted someone he can trust. The fact that this non-agent went out of her way to help him gives him hope that there are people worth trusting. More than that, when she's tested, she protects his mission and saves the day.

My heroine is exactly the kind of person he wants to be with: trustworthy, daring, and even fun. She's always wanted a man who really wants her—who will fight for her and come after her. Luke is exactly this kind of guy when he realizes his feelings for her.

Somewhere in here, you'll have the Black Moment of your story. Then your Epiphany. When you add the Why into the mix, they will also realize what is holding them back from love—their flaws and, perhaps, their lies. In order to win back the one they love, they will embrace the Truth.

This allows them to do the **Big Gesture or Sacrifice,** the thing they do to stay together.

Remember to ask your character: *What is the Big Gesture or Sacrifice they make at the end, for love, that they can't do at the beginning?* It might be letting go if something, or doing something brave, which leads them into the **Happily Ever After,** in which they find the love they've always longed for.

Romances end happily. Even if the hero dies, like *P.S. I Love You*, or *Enemy at the Gates*, or even *Cold Mountain*, they end with an element of happiness, something that makes the reader glad they just spent two days reading your romance! (As opposed to weeping and throwing the book across the room.)

The Notebook works because they are together at the end, even if she is losing her mind. She remembered!

And even ***A Walk to Remember*** works because her love gave him the strength to be a better person and pursue more than he thought possible.

One of my favorite endings is in *Chasing Liberty*—when the heroine goes to London and asks the hero for a ride—just like she did at the beginning of their romance.

We need to believe that the romance has changed them, forever, and made them into better people. **The key is, they have to do something that makes us understand that the romance has impacted them, and they are better off for it.**

So, there you have it, the Act Three Huzzah ending that should make your reader curl up with your book and give a contented sigh (if they are into romance, that is!).

Now you have incorporated the ten ingredients into in your romance. Here's a hint: Put the beats on index cards, and you can move them around to fit your story . . . what you want, when.

Now, write your story summary. No, you don't have all the scenes yet, but you have an idea of where you are going, and all the essential parts to build your romance. As you are writing your synopsis, you also have the "checklist" to make sure you have all your elements.

A romance doesn't have to be complicated, but it does need to fulfill the expectations of the reader.

Boy Meets Girl . . . and they lived Happily Ever After.

And everything in between.

EXTRA GOODIES

The Use of Secondary Characters

I'm important too!

I'm sitting here at my husband's office working on this chapter, and the front desk reception fella (a friend named Jim) asks me, of course, what I'm writing about:

Me: The use of Secondary Characters in a book.
Him: Or misuse. (He's an avid reader.)
Me: (because I haven't had my coffee yet) Huh?
Him: Well, think about it, just the name: Secondary Character. How would you like to be called a *Secondary Character*? They're important too!

He's brilliant! And right! See, Secondary Characters are key to a great story. Think of Watson, to Sherlock Holmes. Harry Potter and Ron Weasley. And Barney Fife to Andy Griffith. Laverne and Shirley. And, Holy Sidekicks, how about Batman and Robin?

The point is, a great character, and a great story, is enhanced by great Secondary Characters.

Who is in your world? We are, in large part, defined by the people we allow into our lives, the people we choose to spend time with, listen to, allow to influence us, and even challenge us. These people help us grow, (even if we make mistakes with them!) and teach more about ourselves, our world, our faith.

Secondary Characters in a novel act the same way. Author Rachel Hauck wrote an excellent article about Secondary Characters in the spring 2011 issue of *Voices*, the MBT e-zine, and with her permission, I'm going to use some of her points here as a starting place.

From Rachel:

"Secondary Characters are critical to every story. Through their eyes, we see the hero and heroine from different angles. Even if a Secondary Character is not a point-of-view (POV) character, his or her dialogue and action can round out the story and the protagonist."

Here is a short list of the benefits of Secondary Characters:

Secondary Characters widen the story – Written too close to the protagonist, a story can feel claustrophobic. By adding a Secondary Character friend or family member, you widen the story's stage. We see beyond the protagonist's heart and mind.

Secondary Characters trigger backstory – Dialogue with Secondary Characters helps deliver the protagonist's past, secrets, or inner thoughts. Don't have your protagonist musing to herself about her past, or that tomorrow is her birthday and everyone seems to have forgotten. Have her talk to a friend, family member, or the regular barista at her favorite coffee shop.

Secondary Characters supply humor – Secondary Characters can be more "off the page" than the main characters. Their problems don't have to go as deep, nor their resolutions as far.

Secondary Characters add conflict – Secondary Characters enter the story just when the protagonist doesn't need or want them. Perhaps they bring an additional problem to our hero or heroine. Worse, a Secondary Character may expose a motive or secret of our protagonist.

Secondary Characters reveal the protagonist – Expose the strengths and weaknesses of the protagonist through the eyes and mouth of a Secondary Character.

And most of all, Secondary Characters **widen the theme of the story.**

More than just people who give the protagonist someone to chat with, they can act as truth tellers, or even catalysts to change in the character's journey. They are, in short, voices of either Reason, or Passion.

What is a Voice of Reason or Passion?

TheVoice of **Passion** lives in my house. She's dressed like my teenage daughter (on any given day that might be a pair of jeans, topped with a skirt, with a tank top under a short-sleeved sweatshirt, and a pair of what my husband calls her Wonder Woman arm protectors). Now, to be fair, my daughter has long moments of what I call sanity, where **Reason** prevails, when I can convince her that no, her brothers aren't trying to drive her crazy, even though they insist on leaving the bathroom . . .well, you know.

And then there are the moments when **Passion** takes over. When, despite our best efforts, life is simply too much, when she must play her music at the top of the allowed decibel levels, when, to put it into *Grey's Anatomy* Speak, she has to dance it out. When that inner wild thing must be heard and set free, just for a moment. Only then can she breathe deeply and restore her sanity.

Sadly, or perhaps comfortingly, I see so much of myself in her. So I know, someday, this too shall pass. (Or not, according to my husband.)

The point is, we all have two sides to ourselves: a Voice of Reason, and a Voice of Passion. All my characters, when I develop them, have said voices, and I use them in various plot points throughout the book. But the fun part is that Secondary Characters are a great way to illustrate the *theme* of the story by making them either a Voice of Reason or a Voice of Passion. Two sides of the character, lived out, so to speak.

Let's say our theme is forgiveness, like it was in my book *Happily Ever After.* Joe, the hero, is grappling with forgiveness, and doesn't know how to forgive someone for something that happened to him. He has a brother who acts as a Voice of Reason, the voice that has perspective and grace and found the right answer.

Also in the story is a villain, someone who is out to sabotage my heroine, Mona. The villain is acting out of unforgiveness, and his anger is causing him to lose his morals, and eventually his freedom. Hmmm . . . sounds like passion out of control to me.

Another example is *The Hunt for Red October.* The central character in the theme is Jack Ryan and the theme is loyalty and trust. Of course, our Voice of Reason is Marko Ramius, a Russian submarine captain who has looked at his life and this silent war and decided to steal a submarine and to escape to the US Eastern Seaboard. And, in the end, decides to trust someone he's never met. The Voice of Passion is the *other* Russian sub commander, who decides *not* to trust his own countrymen, and in fact kill them. (This, of course, makes perfect sense, if you're a Russian sub commander.) But it's two sides to the same theme: How much should you trust someone?

How do you incorporate the Voice of Reason and the Voice of Passion in a book?

1. Start with your theme – What are the two extremes that could be played out? Revenge verses Acceptance? Betrayal versus Loyalty?
2. What would it look like to act out those two extremes in your story?
3. Who could play those roles? (Consider family members, community, friends, even setting.)
4. How could they influence your character to either:
    a. Identify with them?
    b. Reject them?
    (Ideally, both moments should be in the story.)

The Voice of Reason often pops up during Act 2, as that friend who gives the hero or heroine a reality check about the romance. Or is the listening ear at the end that encourages them to pursue their true love. The Voice of Passion often shows up either at the very beginning, as a part of the home world, or Inciting Incident, or it shows up near the Black Moment—perhaps before or after, as a glimpse of how things could have or have gone terribly wrong.

Some powerful Secondary Characters in romance:

In *Return to Me*, Grace has her pal Megan, who helps her weave through the tangles of the romance, playing most often the Voice of Reason.

In *How to Lose a Guy in 10 Days*, Andie finds her friend crying over a broken heart. But it is this friend who helps her see the truth about romance. She is both a Voice of Reason and Passion.

In *A Walk in the Clouds*, Paul's friend is Victoria's grandfather. He knows their secret and tries to help Paul maintain the lie for the family. He is a Voice of Passion telling him to follow true love.

Where to find Secondary Characters:

As you're planning your protagonist and plot, think of those who are involved in your character's life. Consider who might help or hinder him on his journey.

Family – Parents, brothers, and sisters create strong Secondary Characters. They know the protagonist the best and can speak truth or facts that no other character can speak. Use them to deliver key information to the reader about the hero.

Friends – A best friend can be a powerful force in the protagonist's journey. He will often know things about the hero others might not know, including family. A college roommate, a childhood friend, a teammate, or work colleague. Use friends to bring challenge and truth to the hero.

In Siri Mitchell's *She Walks in Beauty*, Lizzie, the best friend of the heroine, Clara, is a source of comfort, truth—and conflict. The friends are eyeing the same man to be their groom.

Society or Community – Who makes up your character's community? Is there a neighbor or coffee barista the protagonist sees on a daily or weekly basis who can speak truth, add humor, or provide a mirror in which readers see the protagonist?

Build in Secondary Characters, and you will not only have a Voice of Reason or Passion, but you'll also have another story to tell. Look for ways you can accentuate the theme, to give it different points of view, and then apply them to your Secondary Characters. Suddenly, they'll have their own voice and meaning on the page. And you'll have made them not a Secondary Character . . . but a **Significant Character**. (Do you like that better, Jim?)

Do you have Secondary Characters in your stories? Are you using them as a Voice of Reason or Passion?

Lethal Weapons in Romance

I'm now going to give away my secrets. Well, not all of them, but the essential ones that will assist you in writing a killer romance. They are what I call…

Lethal Weapons!

These are the elements of a great romance that grab your readers' hearts, leave them weak and unable to put your book down and walk away. These are things that make them weep and fall in love. The elements that wring them out and cause them to go buy more of your books. ☺ Or read the same one over and over.

Hot Dates: Every couple needs to have one great date. I love unique dates. I've had my characters have a picnic at the dump while watching the bears. I've had them play hockey, basketball, and touch football. I've had them go fishing, go blueberry picking, take a drive. I've had them make s'mores, and go to the theater, and ride through Siberia on a snowmobile. The key to this hot date is to get them alone and to create desire. You want them to like being together, and see the potential for true love. But you also want to create tension because even as the Why they should be together grows stronger, the Why Not should also become glaringly painful.

A great date creates more tension, more longing, more anguish. And it makes readers root for true love. We talked about dates in the Wooing section, but be really creative with your dates and make them stand out for your readers.

Love Language: It's the little things that count. Recently my husband gave me a Michael Bublé CD. A small gift, but oh, I love it. I have already worn it out. Why did it mean so much? Because gifts are one of my love languages. Discovering your character's love languages (Time, Affirmation, Gifts, Service, Touch) and having the hero or heroine meet them in small but profound ways creates an impact on readers. It acts as a secret the readers and hero share in the wooing of the heroine (or readers and heroine). The readers know what is going on, if only the heroine would wake up and see it! It's a delicious little lethal weapon that builds the bond between readers and the characters and deepens the magic of the romance.

Secrets: Don't you just love it when someone tells you a secret? Something private that only you two share? Your hero and heroine have secrets too. When you share them with your readers, it builds the bond. Not only that, but when the hero and heroine then share the secret with the other, readers participate in the sharing (or the receiving). Secrets bond characters together, and bond readers to characters. Need a hint on finding a secret? Go back to that dark place in your hero's and heroine's past and pull something from that. And, if you want, you can share it on the Hot Date! (Or, even better, after a painful argument!)

Longings: *What if. . .Don't you just wish that. . .If only. . .* When someone shares with you that deepest desire of their heart, you get a glimpse of their soul. I love knowing the longings of the people I love because maybe I can participate in fulfilling them. Even if I can't, it makes me understand them and like them more. Your hero and heroine must share their deepest longings with readers, and each other. It's a moment that will make your readers fall in love with the heart of your characters.

Keeping the Romance Alive

Think back to the days when you were first falling in love. It wasn't long after you met that you began to think about your new romance. Perhaps you started by detouring to the coffee shop about the same time he did. Or you started eating lunches in the company lunchroom. Perhaps you began to check your Facebook, e-mail and voice mail more regularly. You cleared out spots on your calendar, perhaps even when you went to the store you considered your new romance's tastes when shopping for clothes, food, music. With each step in the romance, your thoughts toward each other filled more of your lives until every moment overflowed with thoughts about your new love.

Your romance novel should play out the same way. As the romance thread grows, it takes up more time in the novel as well as makes a more profound impact on your hero and heroine's decisions. We've talked about how to grow your romance through the scenes, kisses and powerful dialogue, but the other essential way to grow the romance and keep it alive is by **putting the romance on every page.**

Often novelists believe that this means having the hero and heroine physically together on every page. However, this may be a challenge (and unrealistic) based on your plot. One trick to keeping them together is to start with sprinkling thoughts the hero and heroine have for each other onto the pages.

Consider this: Just like when you first meet someone, they might be intriguing, but you don't spend every moment thinking about them. However, they enter your thoughts when appropriate—when you are reminded of something they said or did. In the same way, as you begin your romance, the hero and heroine should make an impact on the other in a way that brings them to mind. In this way, you light the romance fires and move them naturally into a deeper relationship.

Keeping the romance fires lit on every page is all about showing how the romance increasingly impacts every area of the POV character's life so that when they break up, it isn't just sad, it's devastating.

Try this: **As you write the scene, ask:** Are my hero or heroine physically together in the scene? If they aren't, what elements in the scene cause them to think about each other? Does the hero or heroine make decisions based on the current status of the romance (negative or positive)?

Note: if you have gone through an entire scene without the hero or heroine characters contemplating or interacting with their relationship with the other in some way, the romance hasn't made enough impact on the character . . . or the reader. It's time for a rewrite.

A powerful romance isn't just about structure—it's about drawing the hero and heroine closer, impacting each other's life, and thereby, your readers' lives.

My Book is Finished. Now What?

Now that you have something to work with, let's talk about editing. See, you can't edit something that *isn't there*. Think of editing as taking that rough form and making a masterpiece out of it.

I like to get the entire story on the page and write the entire book before I edit. Some authors, however, like to edit as they go. But be warned: You can really get caught up in editing. It's easier, in some ways, than writing, because the words are already there. You don't have to create. So, make some limits for yourself. Do only one or two editing passes before you force yourself to keep going. You can always come back later and re-edit. If you edit after you're farther in the story, you'll discover new elements and textures you want to add to your previous chapters.

Editing

Editing, in my opinion, is the fun part of writing. You already have the rough draft nailed down, and now you're going to hone it, add all those things that will make it sparkle.

For me, there are three phases to writing a book:

1. **Creating** – The long, painful discovery of the scenes. Again, keep a notebook of all the things you want to put in it later during the:

2. **Revision phase** – It's the phase where I hone the theme and add special elements, like the five senses, or thematic metaphors. I draw out scenes that need to be longer, shorten ones that are too long, even delete unnecessary scenes. This is where I add character textures such as:
   - ✓ *Idiosyncrasies – mannerisms, something the character says out of habit*
   - ✓ *Food and drink preferences*
   - ✓ *Clothing and kind of car*
   - ✓ *Nicknames (my secret weapon)*

   Which leads us to the:

3. **Editing phase** – Print your scene out and read it slowly, taking notes in the lines, proofing it, and going through my checklist. (See below.)

Editing Checklist:

What to look for when editing:

- ✓ **Scenes that pack a punch** – Do each of your scenes have a purpose? Do you need to make the slower scenes faster? Can you combine two slow scenes, cutting away the less important to the important?
- ✓ **Action** – Are there sufficient reasons for everything your character does in that scene? Have you planted the clues for that action or decision long before they do it?
- ✓ **Likeable characters** – Do your hero and heroine have great qualities that make you truly like them? Make sure that in each scene, there is something likeable about your characters—that special spark that sets them apart.
- ✓ **Surprise** – Don't give us an expected plot. Are the plot points, the scenes cliff hangers, the romantic obstacles plausible yet unexpected?
- ✓ **Art** – Have you mastered the mechanics?

Mechanics Overview

1. Are there five senses in each scene?

2. Replace the adverbs with strong verbs, the adjectives with defined nouns. Cut all "ly" ending adverbs if possible.

3. Be ruthless with passive sentences. "Was" and "were," "has been" and "have been," are good clues to a passive sentence. Although sometimes you need a passive sentence to let the reader rest, most of your sentences should be active.

4. Repeating sentences – If two sentences say virtually the same thing, cut one.

5. Two adjectives together weaken both. Use the strongest one.

6. Read through your dialogue – Do you need tags? Do you have enough action between words? Do you repeat names? Do you need to delete tags to make it faster? Is there enough white space between chunks of dialogue? Body language? Fighting words?

7. Do you have a list of overused words? Do a word search and fix/delete those!

Now, what is the difference between *strengthening* a scene and *re-arranging* the words? Strengthening a scene is discovering the emotional significance to the scene, the way it will affect the overall book, and milking it for the reader. Using setting and dialogue and body language and disappointment and *words* to cut to the heart of a character.

Rearranging words, on the other hand, is merely putting them in a different order. Ordering them differently. Rearranging them so they say that same thing, only in a different way. Maybe even going on and on and on about the same thing in hopes of driving your point home . . . . ☺

PUTTING IT ALL TOGETHER: WRITING THE SYNOPSIS

So, you've written your book, edited it, and now it's time to submit your book!

Okay, wait, maybe that proclamation was premature. I got a little excited there. First you need to write a Proposal, which consists of a cover or query letter (depending on what your prospective publisher wants to see first), a synopsis, and the first three chapters of your novel.

I like to write my cover or query letter *last*, because, well, by then I know what I'm trying to say.

And, you should have written those first three chapters, right? (Because, well, you've also typed, "The End.")

So, let's talk a little about the **synopsis**.

We've talked about all the ingredients you'll need for your Romance. You know who your characters are, what stands between them and true love, and how love will win the day. Now, it's time to tell the world.

A synopsis is nothing more than a summary of your story. Go back to your ten ingredients, put them in the order you will use them, then use the following steps to weave these ingredients into a synopsis.

> **Step One:** A good synopsis starts out with outlining the characters' deepest desires. What are they after, and why? What will they learn? What do they want, and why? What is their conflict?
>
> **Step Two:** Move the story through the obstacles. Highlight some of the things that your characters will struggle with, internally and romantically (spiritually and emotionally.) Use the physical plot points to jump from paragraph to paragraph, writing it in proper POV.
>
> Note: A synopsis is supposed to be an **Overview** of the story. One mistake I see made by beginning writers is the tendency to narrow in on the details. You want to step back from the story and squint a little and tell us the big events you see, and how they affect the spiritual and emotional threads. Don't tell us how he stops and caresses her hand as he

declares his love. Just say, "He declares his love." Details slow the pace and will make the editor put the synopsis down. You don't want this to happen.

Hook your editor and bring him/her through the story, holding her breath, until you end with:

Step Three: Tie up the synopsis nicely by telling us how the title or theme fits in to your story, wrapping it up like a gift for your reader.

Don't worry about length, or style, just spit it out. We're not looking for a polished piece yet. You just want to tell the story. Shoot for three to five pages, and stick to the main plot. Your goal is to wind all the threads through the story, beginning to end. For now, just get it down on paper.

But what about those chapter-by-chapter summaries? Yes, there are a few publishers who want a chapter break-down. Don't panic. This is similar to a synopsis in that it includes desires, obstacles, and conflicts. It simply breaks them apart for each chapter.

Here's a secret: I often write both a synopsis and a chapter-by-chapter summary, even if my publisher only asks for one of them. I find the chapter-by-chapter summary serves as a roadmap for my book, and when I sit down to write it, I have a jumpstart on my creativity for that chapter. A synopsis is more entertaining, and a good way to introduce your writing style to your editor. But a chapter-by-chapter summary is more detailed, and proves you have your plot figured out. My suggestion: Try writing both!

Make It Colorful

A synopsis is not only the summary of your story. Like I said, it is a slice of your writing style. It gives the editor the first taste of who you are and what you write. Because of that, you want to give the synopsis the flavor of the type of story you write.

What do I mean? Well, we talked about how every noun and verb you use conveys a feeling or mood in a scene. For example, if you are trying to up tension and create fear, you might use verbs that generate feelings of fear, e.g., *stricken, caught, blindsided, choked.*

If you want to convey feelings of warmth, you might use *embraced, soothe, coo.* If you want to create feelings of suspense, you might use *flicker, ripped, tear.*

The idea is to look at your manuscript, and handpick the words you use to convey the mood and to illuminate the story. Then, use them when writing your synopsis. Why not? You want to create a mood for your synopsis, too, right?

Here are the first three paragraphs of the synopsis for my Deep Haven book, *The Perfect Match.* It is about the sparks that fly when the new lady fire chief falls for the town pastor. Let's start with the basic synopsis, without the colorful words.

> Ellie Karlson really wants to be a good firefighter. She's found a job in a small town and if she does really well, she'll not only be the permanent chief, but she'll also feel like she's somehow made up for causing the death of her brother. What she doesn't know is that there is someone setting fires in town and she'll have to catch him if she wants to keep her job. The lessons she learns about God in the process will change her life.
>
> Dan Matthews is tired of ministry. He needs help. But who can he look to? He desires a wife, but doesn't know the kind of wife God wants for him. On the night when one of his parishioners dies, he meets the new first chief, Ellie Karlson, and starts to wonder if she is the one God picked out. Can he sense God's will?

These paragraphs tell the basics, why Ellie wants to succeed, why Dan wants a wife. However, they don't have spark and sizzle.

Now, here's the synopsis with the color words added. I'm going to bold the words I use to convey mood.

> Ellie Karlson just **landed** her dream job . . . or so she thinks. In town to **helm** the three-month interim position of Fire Chief for the Deep Haven volunteer fire department, she has big plans to turn this into a permanent gig. It's taken fifteen years to finally fill the shoes her brother left behind with his untimely death, and she isn't going to let prejudice, an arsonist, or the chauvinistic town pastor keep her from her goals. But the job she's **sacrificed** for is about to **cost** more than she expects. Only by turning to God and **holding on tight** will she **survive**.
>
> Pastor Dan Matthews is feeling **burned out** in ministry. After three years at the helm of Grace Church in Deep Haven, he has serious **doubts** that his preaching or his attempts at discipleship are **bearing fruit** in the spiritual landscape of his congregation. Feeling like a failure, he can't help but wonder if firefighting is a better job. At least it has instant results. Maybe what he needs is a partner in ministry—a wife, a helper, just as God designed, to **ease the load**. On the night when all his losses seem to **flash over**, he meets a woman who can only be from his dreams, and he can't help but wonder if God has heard his silent prayers.
>
> **Then the smoke clears**. Ellie Karlson may be a cute **fireball of energy**, but she's certainly not his picture of a helpmeet. She may be able to **haul hose** faster than any man in town, and know how to **chop down** a door with an axe, but last time he looked, those abilities weren't on his "perfect wife" qualifications. If only she didn't **light his heart on fire and ignite**, for the first time, the missing passion in his soul for life and ministry.

Try this: Go through your synopsis and for each verb or noun, see if you can rework or find a way to make it stronger, add mood, and give it punch.

Query Letters

Now that you are making your synopsis colorful and packing it with a punch, you only have two more aspects of your proposal to put together: your query letter and sample chapters.

A query letter may be sent separately, before you send in your entire proposal, or it may take the form of a cover letter. It can be sent via e-mail or hard copy. Always check to make sure your intended recipient—agent or editor—accepts e-mail queries. A query letter is your pitc pitch: the what, why, and hows of your story.

What makes a good query letter?

1. A compelling, succinct first paragraph hook.
2. A summary of your book in two to three sentences.
3. An explanation of where your manuscript fits into the publishing world.
4. Who you are and why you can successfully pull off this book.
5. The mechanics of the manuscript—where you're at in production.

The Hook:
In my opinion, the most important part of the query letter is the beginning hook. This is where you get the editor's attention, the part that will keep him or her from tossing all your hard work into the circular file. Consider how many proposals channel through an editor's hands in one month. This thought alone should impress you with the importance of the hook.

1. What is a hook?
It's the Who, What, and Why of the story. It's the juiciest tidbit, the selling aspect that makes *your* story different from the rest. This is where you take your knockout paragraph, boil it down to the *most* important aspect, and highlight it. You want to create questions and interest. You should do this in less than 100 words.

For example, in my query letter for *Happily Ever After*, I wrote:

Mona Reynolds longs for two things: forgiveness and Jonah, the hero from her favorite book. But getting either is about as likely as her father rising from the dead. Instead, she runs home, to Deep Haven, MN, to open her dream bookstore. Joe Michaels has never stopped running. He is merely slowing down to visit a brother he barely knows. When Mona's dreams begin to crumble, Joe is conveniently there to save her. But when dreams turn to disaster, is Joe the man she hopes he is? Or is he someone much, much different?

The key here is to *not* give away the details, but to think like a marketing person and find the juiciest tidbits. Think of the blurbs on the back of books. They grab you, and much of the time, based on that 100 word summary, you purchase the book. That is the response you're aiming for.

2. Summarizing your book.
What are the theme and the take-away message of your book? You must get very creative, descriptive, and frugal in this section of your query letter. The key is to say as much as possible about the book, in terms of its content, in two to four sentences. Query letters should be one page only. The editor just doesn't have time to read more than that.

Here is what I wrote for *Happily Ever After*:

Through a myriad of disasters, including a family of roaches, a house fire, a saboteur, and finally the unveiling of Joe's secrets, Joe and Mona discover that when they turn their hopes over to the Lord, He will satisfy their wildest dreams and fulfill the longings of their hearts.

3. Where does your book fit in the market?
Is your book a stand alone? The first in a series? Why is it unique? This is the paragraph where you really sell your book. Go ahead, tell the editor why it is great, and tell him or her where it will fit in their lineup. Definitely do some research and know what the publisher offers. *Don't* try and sell a romance to a publisher who doesn't publish romance. Then, pump up those traits your book has, the ones you know they want.

Here is my marketing paragraph. Note that I am selling the series, as well as book one.

Set in the fictional, picturesque tourist town of Deep Haven, northern Minnesota, *Happily Ever After* is the first in a three-part collection entitled, "The Deep Haven Series." Each book tells the story of a woman, running from the storms of life and searching for a home, who discovers true love and the inner peace that only a deep relationship with God can bring. The series combines the threads of mystery, suspense, and spiritual searching with heartwarming tales of love, and weaves them into satisfying romances set in a town we'd all love to visit. Attached is a short summary of the series and the titles in the collection.

4. Who are you and why can you write this book?
In one or two sentences, highlight your publishing credits. If you don't have any, list the reasons why you are an authority to write this story. Obviously, I could pull off Russian stories with some degree of authenticity because of my missionary experience. And my first book with Tyndale was a "found my true love in Russia" story. I spent my childhood in an idyllic town in northern Minnesota, so I was able to write with some legitimacy about the state's north shore.

Here's my authority statement:

I am a missionary in Far East Russia, who grew up on the beautiful north shore of Minnesota. I've published numerous devotionals and articles, and this story won first place in an online contest.

5. The mechanics.
This paragraph simply explains how long the book is, how much you have written, whether your proposal is out to other publishers as well, and details the items you've included in your package. And, of course, don't forget to thank the editor for his or her time in reading the proposal.

Here's how I finished my query letter:

Happily Ever After is a completed manuscript of 90,000 words. Currently, this is a simultaneous submission. (Note: "Simultaneous submission" means you've sent the manuscript to other editors and/or agents at the same time. Check your each publisher's or agent's policy on this.) Attached please find the story synopsis and the first three chapters. Thank you for your consideration.

Those are the basics of a good query letter.

In short, the query letter hooks your editor on your idea and the synopsis hooks them on your ability to weave a story. And, of course, the sample chapters hook them on your writing ability.

A Word about Sample Chapters

Your proposal is nearly finished! You have your well-threaded synopsis, knockout first paragraph, and a compelling query letter that hooks your editor. Now, all you need are the sample chapters!

Sample Chapters:
Every proposal package includes sample chapters for the story you are proposing. Even if you are a multi-published author, you will have to write sample chapters for new contracts with new publishers, so it is wise to learn how to write them now.

When new authors read "Sample Chapters" in the submission requirements of an editor's or publisher's website, sometimes they are tempted to think, "I'll pick my *best* chapters: chapter one, chapter eight, and chapter twenty-two." Delete that thought. Editors *do not* want to see a set of random chapters. They want to see the *first three chapters.* They want to see how the story flows, they want to hear your voice, and they want to know how you develop characters. So, when you see the words "Sample Chapters," think: first three chapters. If you have a *short* prologue, you can include it. If, however, you have a prologue that is five pages long (and really, you shouldn't, but that's another discussion), include it as one of your first three chapters.

Think of the synopsis as your editor's first introduction to your writing, the teaser, so to speak. The sample chapters make an editor fall in love with your style.

When you prepare your sample chapters, refer to the publisher's guidelines to know how to format it. Some want a specific type style and margins. Always put a header on the top left with your name and the name of the manuscript. Add the page number in the upper right hand corner.

I usually spend at least two weeks on my sample chapters, making sure they are compelling, introduce enough conflict, and make the editor want to turn the page. It pays to take the time to get it right, so don't rush it. Usually it takes me one month to compile a good proposal. One week for market research, another two for sample chapter polish, and one more for synopsis and query polish. Don't rush it. Once an editor reviews your work, if he or she turns it down, it is hard to get a second chance.

THE BUSINESS SIDE OF WRITING ROMANCE

The writer's life is at once exciting and lonely. No one else is inside your brain with you as you create. No one else feels the same triumph when you get the scene right, or when your characters are finally overcoming their trials. I have a friend who calls me and occasionally she'll hear a long silence and know that I'm in the middle of a big scene. She's a good enough friend to say, "Uh, I'll call you later."

I'm a huge fan of finding a writing partner to journey with you. Not a critique partner, but a craft partner, someone who will commit with you to helping each other become better at craft elements (dialogue, storyworld, hook, emotional layering, etc.). Critique partners often have different voices, and may critique a manuscript based on their own tastes. A craft partner, however, focuses on developing writing skills and allows the voice of a writer to flourish.

How do you find such a partner? There are a number of romance communities starting with the largest, the Romance Writer's of America (RWA). (www.rwa.org). They have a national organization as well as a yearly conference. In addition, they have chapters all over the world where a writer might find community for general romance writing. Furthermore, they have chapters for particular genres, both online and offline, and host one of the most prestigious writer's contests: the RITA awards. Membership is annual.

If you tend toward a more inspirational taste in your romance, I highly recommend the American Christian Fiction Writers (ACFW). (www.acfw.org). Originally started as the American Christian Romance Writers, it's the largest community for inspirational novelists in the world, and many of their members write romance. They have many of the same benefits as RWA, including local chapters and an annual conference. ACFW membership is also annual.

Both the above organizations provide essential information about the publishing industry. RWA focuses on the ABA (general market books) while ACFW focuses on CBA (the inspirational market). They also offer online classes and articles on writing on their website.

If you are interested in more hands-on coaching and lessons on writing, My Book Therapy (MBT) (www.mybooktherapy.com) offers a free forum for writers, and added benefits (weekly encouragement, monthly lessons, quarterly seminars) for a small monthly membership fee.

I highly recommend joining all three organizations in order to stay on top of your writing career. You'll network, discover new writing opportunities, make friends (and find craft partners!) and expand your knowledge base. Take it a step further and attend at least one retreat or writers conference. That's where networking really begins. Making a commitment in your writing by joining a professional organization is a giant and beneficial leap to becoming a professional writer.

Now, how about some Q&A?

Q: *There are so many kinds of books out there, and it seems each publisher wants a different thing. Where do I start?*

A: Work with publishers who are willing to work with you.

There are many publishers out there who are thrilled to work with new writers—and the list is growing. Harlequin is one of the most popular ways authors get started because they embrace new authors, and love to groom them. They also publish a slew of books every month in their different 'category' romance lines. Go to Wal-Mart and check out their current releases to see where you might fit in. These books often also go to the "club" readers, or those who subscribe to their category line. This is a great place to begin because they get your books out to a target market who loves to read the genre they order. Not only do you gain experience, but a readership. And it's very fun to walk into a Wal-Mart and see your book sitting on the shelf. These novels usually run 55-60K words.

But, you say, my book is much longer than 55,000 words!

You may want to submit to a trade publisher, someone who publishes longer books. (Most publishers are trade). They may still put them out in mass market size (the size you see on your grocery store rack), but they are not a part of a publisher's "club" line. Trade sized books are the size you might see in a library, or on a bookstore shelf. Publishers of books are always putting out their "we're looking for" lists—and you can keep up to date on these via RWA, ACFW, or other industry organizations. (Attending a conference publishing panel is an essential part of keeping track of what publishers are looking for.)

Regardless of what kind of book you are writing, there are two main ways to build your career:

Route 1: Snowball to success. Maybe you have started with a Heartsong book, and grew a readership. Maybe you're also selling to Love Inspired. (Many, many authors make a great living selling to just those two lines. They have devoted readers and are reaching people every day.) You could stop there. Or, because that science fiction novel is still in your heart, and because of your numbers and experience you land an agent—and he finds a market that publishes sci-fi. You finally sell the book of your dreams.

Route 2: Go for the big bang. With this route, you work on that manuscript for years and years, submitting that sci-fi, waiting for the market to open, honing your work, winning contests, submitting to agents. You finally get an agent who sees the vision of your story, and you listen to what they say until you get a manuscript they can sell. Then your agent submits it around and—finally!—the sci-fi publisher buys it.

Kiss and Tell!

So there you have it: the step by step instructions to writing a powerful romance, from plotting to word-smithing to secrets. I hope this book has been helpful. Drop me a line and tell me about your book. Andif you need some personal one-on-one help, check out My Book Therapy. We'll help you discover the writer in you!

I want to leave you with *one last secret*:

***The My Book Therapy Secret Formula for a Bestselling Romance*!**

- ✓ Powerful Why Nots to keep the characters apart.
- ✓ Compelling Whys to why they belong together.
- ✓ Multifaceted characters with humorous and endearing quirks, revealed layer by layer.
- ✓ Realistic plot with make-it-worse for them elements on all levels: physical, spiritual, emotional (and a happy ending).
- ✓ Storyworld that makes you feel the scene and sense the mood.
- ✓ Backstory in small pieces, culminating to the final scene.
- ✓ Well-researched details that make the story and characters realistic.
- ✓ Heart-wrenching break up and a sweet Happily Ever After.
- ✓ Truth message that touches the heart.

Now it's time for you to . . . Kiss and Tell!

Happy Writing!

Susie May Warren

Appendix: Story Structure

Note: If you are not familiar with basic story structure, refer to Appendix 1. You may also want to pick up a copy of *From the Inside . . . Out: discover, create and publish the novel in you*!

THE BASIC PLOT

Because I'm a gal who loves lists, I've come up with an acrostic to help you keep your plot straight. And, hey, let's have a little fun and dance our way through the discovery.

Every book has a three-act structure, with the first being the introductory and set-up, the middle being the "guts," and the final act being the "glory," or Big Finale.

Act 1:

- ✓ *Life or Normal World* – This is the world in which your character normally lives. Their challenges, their status quo. Sometimes this is a chapter long, maybe longer, although more and more, it's shortening to the first few pages. It gives us a glimpse of their regular life.
- ✓ *Inciting Incident* – Something happens. Some writing classes call it the *trigger* or *ignition.* But it's the first blip in their world, big or small, that will change it and set them on the course of their journey.
- ✓ *Noble Quest* – The effect of the Inciting Incident is to start a quest. In the case of an unpleasant Inciting Incident, the quest is to return to the normal world. In a positive Inciting Incident, the quest is to increase that pleasure. In either quest, the hero must recognize what's at stake. The higher the stakes to person, family, community, country, or world, the bigger the story, the broader the reader base.

Act 2:

- ✓ *Disappointments* – These are the obstacles and conflicts the hero encounters. Even positive events can rumple the advancement of the plot. It may be caused by a revelation of information, or because of a choice, or because of outside forces. But the Disappointment has to contain two elements:
  - o *Unexpectedness* – Don't foreshadow the surprise too much or you will disappoint your reader.
  - o *Plausibility* – It has to be in the bounds of credibility.

- ✓ *Y in the Road* – Or "What am I going to do now?" Every character reaches a point where they have to make a choice about their actions. Do they quit? Is it worth the cost? Do they go forward? Often, the best stories include two equally worthy choices, and the character is forced to choose between external goals and internal goals. Their choice, however, will spark new conflicts and, eventually, they reach the point of no return. A good Y in the Road must involve:
  - o *Consequences* – A plot must allow for a character's choices, and then consequences for those choices. Preferably, the character's choice lands them in a worse situation and leads to their darkest point.

- *Surprises* – These come up as the character continues to make choices in the middle act of the story, each one testing their mettle more and more.

Act 3:

- ✓ *Help!* Or *Climax* – This is the final challenge, the event that the book has been building to. The character's goal is usually in jeopardy, and everything they've worked for is at stake. There is *no hope.* This is the Black Moment, where it seems that it can't get any worse. Often a character's Epiphany occurs right before or right after the Climax.
- ✓ *Overhaul* – This is the change that occurs in the character, something internal or external, something that redefines them, and something logical that is derived from the journey.
- ✓ *Perfect Ending Resolution* – The new status quo, the new normal. This is when the character reaches the goal. As you write, keep in mind there must be an end game, something definable to the reader, and the character.

> *The Basic Plot Structure*
>
> *Life* – Once Upon a Time
> *Inciting Incident* – Something out of the ordinary happens
> *Noble Quest* – Causing the protagonist to seek something
> *Disappointment* –But things don't go as expected
> *Y in the Road* – Forcing the protagonist to make a difficult decision
> *Help* – Which has consequences
> *Overhaul* –The result of which is a changed person
> *Perfect Ending* – And they all lived happily ever after (or didn't!)

Just starting on your novel?

Get the writing work-text designed to help you create the novel you've always wanted to write!

From the Inside . . . Out:
discover, create and publish the novel in you!

Always wanted to write a novel but didn't know where to start? This book is for you! Step by step lessons, techniques, explanations, and exercises to get your novel from an idea to the page written by your Book Therapists Susan May Warren & Rachel Hauck.

"A quirky, fun, practical guide from two writers who know what they're doing." -- **James Scott Bell, bestselling author of *Write Great Fiction: Plot & Structure.***

Deep and Wide:
Advanced fiction techniques for making your characters deeper and your plot wider.

The follow-up work-text to *From the Inside . . . Out: discover, create and publish the novel in you!*, *Deep and Wide* utilizes Susan May Warren's easy to apply explanations, exercises, and intuitive methods to teach advanced fiction techniques that will turn any novel from boring to . . . breathtaking.

"If you're intending to write a best-selling novel, I can think of no better place to start than with Susan May Warren's Deep and Wide. *This is a book for those who need to dig into the techniques of writing -- not just hear the happy-talk, big-picture stuff that is so often heard at conferences. If you really want to get into the nuts and bolts of writing strong fiction, then this is for you. Clearpractical advice from an award-winning novelist."* – Chip MacGregor, Literary Agent, MacGregor Literary

The Book Buddy: Your Manuscript Companion

You've got a friend in me . . .

He doesn't fetch coffee or make cookies.
He just helps make your writing dreams come true.

The writing journey can be long and lonely. It's easy to get lost in the weeds of your story, not sure where you are headed . . . or why. Wouldn't it be nice to have a guide along the way, someone to point you in right direction, keep you motivated?

Your *Book Buddy* is here.

A manuscript companion to the foundational writer's work-text: *From the Inside . . . Out: discover, create and publish the novel in you*, and the advanced fiction writer's worktext: *Deep and Wide*, *The Book Buddy* puts feet to all the steps needed to create a powerful book, guiding you through character creation, plotting the inner and outer journey, creating essential scenes, and word painting. It helps you craft the perfect Black Moment, and pushes you on all the way to the climatic ending.

"***The Book Buddy*** is my new best friend! It takes all of the helpful tools, charts and tips from *Inside Out* and *Deep and Wide* and puts them in one place. It's like having Susan May Warren in the room helping you craft your story! I can't recommend it highly enough!" Melissa Tagg, 2010 Frasier Winner

"The Book Buddy is a one-of-a-kind workbook for writers! Jam-packed with questions and charts to help you outline your next book, ***The Book Buddy*** is the next best thing to having award-winning author Susan May Warren willing to devote hours each day to sit beside you and coach you while you write." ~Beth K. Vogt, author and editor

Want to keep on top of the writing industry?
Join the MBT Team!

CRAFT

Over 500 articles on writing craft, industry, marketing, and the writing life
- Basic Publishing Articles
- The Hero's Journey Simplified
- Blog-A-Book – How to develop a story and write a proposal
- Kiss and Tell – How to write a romance
- Sneak and Peak – How to write a Suspense
- Discounts on MBT Products – books and writing helps

COACHING

- Monthly Seminars
- Weekly Chats on craft and interviews with industry professionals
- Weekly Writer's Challenge
- Weekly Writing encouragement
- Monthly Team Member newsletter on how to edit your book into publication
- Discounts on the MBT Retreats
  - The Storycrafter's Retreat – Minneapolis, MN, October.
  - The Deep Thinker's Retreat – Florida, February
  - The Pitch and Promotion Seminar- Before ACFW, September

COMMUNITY

- Discussion Boards
- The Frasier Contest
- The MBT Voices E-zine – an opportunity to get published!
- Annual Pizza Party
- Local writing craft groups

Go to: www.mybooktherapy.com to find out how to join the Team!